God's Voice to
Today's America

GOD'S WARNING TO THE WORLD

BOOK II

Compiled from speeches given by
Reverend Sun Myung Moon

God's Voice to Today's America

GOD'S WARNING TO THE WORLD

BOOK II

Compiled from speeches given by
Reverend Sun Myung Moon

ISBN 0-910621-45-4

**The Holy Spirit Association for the
Unification of World Christianity.**
4 West 43rd Street
New York, N.Y. 10036

Produced by **Accord Inc.**

First Printing 1985

Printed in the United States of America

Contents

Introduction

If any man would come after me, let him deny himself and take up his cross and follow me. For who ever would save his life will lose it; and whoever loses his life for my sake and the gospel's will save it.
Mark 8:34-35

When Sun Myung Moon came to America in 1972, he came as a prophet of God, called to preach a message of revival in the face of rejection and persecution. His message was controversial, and his intentions have been frequently misunderstood and misrepresented, yet nothing deterred him from speaking out. The public ridicule by the media and other groups has never hindered Rev. Moon, because he sincerely believes that he is doing the work of God and that God is assisting his work. When, in 1982, Rev. Moon voluntarily returned from Korea to face charges of tax evasion, he came knowing that he faced an embarrassing trial and possible imprisonment yet was determined to bear that burden if it was necessary for the fulfillment of God's work in America. In spite of the verdict and the refusal of the Supreme Court to hear his appeal, his prayer to God was always, "What way do You want to lead us now? What is Your next chapter for me? Let Your will be done."

As Rev. Moon departed for Danbury prison, he declared that his faith would never change, and that despite this new cross, he would continue to work for the fulfillment of God's will, for the unity of Christianity and the revival of God's spirit in America. Consistent with his pledge, in the winter of 1984-1985 he sent out 300,000 videotapes and literature sets to ministers all across America. Included in that material was a book, *God's Warning to the World*, which was a strong prophetic message to America and Christianity. That message from prison was a warning to America, given out of love, that it has not yet lived up to God's expectation. Rev. Moon believes that American Christians should set an example of goodness, righteousness, and sacrificial love for the world. He is concerned that a self-centered, materialistic America is liable to God's judgment, while salvation lies in living out the teachings and spirit of Jesus Christ.

This second book in the series continues and expands upon the message of *God's Warning to the World*. While the first book centers around the themes of God's expectation for America and the providential role of Christianity at this time in history, Book Two focuses upon the Christian life and the responsibilities of those who would call Jesus their master and take up his cross.

I have known Rev. Moon for over 27 years, and I can say without reservation that he regards Jesus Christ as his teacher and exemplar. As you may have heard or read, when Rev. Moon was sixteen years old, Jesus appeared to him and commissioned him to do God's work. From that time on, Jesus has been his constant companion, guiding him and assisting the work to its fruition. He himself has emphasized that the Unification Church is not established by Rev. Moon, but by God, using Rev. Moon as His instrument. Actually, without God's support it would have been impossible for the Unification Church to even survive, because it has undergone such serious persecution throughout its history. Even well-intentioned Christians, misunderstanding Rev. Moon's motivation and the circumstances of our church life, have opposed its work. In the face of tremendous obstacles, I believe that it is only because God and Jesus approve of the church and its work that we have survived and continue to develop.

How does Rev. Moon view God, Jesus, and Christianity? Unlike many people today, Rev. Moon does not see God as being merely a human concept or phenomenon. God is a living God who is actively a part of our human life, and the affairs of the world cannot be considered without taking into account the presence of the living God as a primary Actor. At the same time, humans are responsible for their actions. While they often do evil, God chooses, for the purpose of preserving human dignity, not to interfere. Through study of the Bible and through his own prayer, Rev. Moon realized that God was not only a real Person, but also that God's heart is filled with intense pain because human beings have often not understood God's situation and have acted in ways that have brought suffering to themselves and to others. In other words, God is truly our Parent who loves all human beings as His children. He suffers with our pain, rejoices with our deeds of goodness, and unceasingly guides our growth towards the full potential of the divine image. Once he realized that God's heart grieves over the miserable situation of this world, Rev. Moon has unceasingly prayed with tears. If you ever have a chance to listen to one of his prayers, though you may not understand the Korean words, you may perceive the depth of his communication with God even from the tone of his voice.

As for Jesus, Rev. Moon believes that he was a true man. Because the Christ was a real person, his life must be a model for our own lives of faith. God fully revealed Himself in the man Jesus Christ, but what this means is that Jesus, because of his sinlessness, was able to enter into a perfect relationship with God, and so was the first true man. Indeed, Jesus reveals the true human being that each of us may ultimately become. The true person walks with God, feels the heart of God, and works with God to solve the problems of the world. God should be as close as one's own mind.

Who is the true Christian? Today Christianity is divided into countless quarreling sects and denominations, each with its distinctive doctrines and rites, but how many Christians are fervently devoting themselves to the will of God? Rev. Moon believes that deeds, not mere words, are the measure of a person's faith. Jesus lived the model Christian life. He lived for others, even giving his life on the cross that others might have salvation. The true Christian is not known by the orthodoxy of his doctrines, but by his deeds of love and service for God and humankind. That is why Jesus said that anyone who would follow him must deny himself and take up his cross. It is in loving God and loving others that we find God and fellowship with Jesus Christ.

Although Rev. Moon has never had any formal theological training, his ideas and teachings come from many years of intense study of the Bible and tearful prayers full of desperation to know and do God's will.

He is a serious man of faith and prayer. Perhaps the image most deeply engraved in my heart, from my own experiences, is the image of him kneeling in prayer, with tears streaming down his face. I have witnessed his spiritual life for many years, and I know him to be a righteous man who literally weeps for the suffering of God, the suffering of the world, and the speedy establishment of peace and the Kingdom of God on this earth.

Unification Church members have found in Rev. Moon an example of a saintly life; they see him as walking in the footsteps of Jesus Christ and dedicated to the same purpose. Some of you may have met one of the young or not-so-young people of the Unification Church; you might sense a difference in them from other people. They have a spirit of freshness and diligence; they have an attitude of service and tolerance; and their spiritual lives are devout and faithful. Their primary allegiance is not to the man Rev. Moon, but to God and God's will; that is what Rev. Moon has taught them. When they meet you, who are ministers of the Gospel, they view you as fellow workers in Christ. If one should visit your church he might be eager to share his message with you, but you can also teach him what you know and make him a better Christian.

Rev. Moon has been prolific in his output of ideas and inspiration while in prison at Danbury. Daily he continues to teach and share his wisdom. His vision is to comfort the grieving heart of God and end humanity's suffering by reviving the Christian spirit in America, so that America can fulfill her proper leadership role in the world. He recognizes three major obstacles to God's kingdom which need to be confronted and overcome: immorality, disunity of the churches, and the spread of communism.

The first obstacle is the prevalence of immorality, sexual promiscuity, and self-centered love. The ways of promiscuity and immorality lead to attitudes of non-commitment and disrespect for other people and things. Free sex, drug abuse, child abuse, rape, vandalism and murder are just some of the results of this attitude of disrespect and lack of commitment. The numbers of divorces and unstable marriages are increasing as each generation fails to understand the value of long-lasting commitments and self-sacrifice for the sake of others. Unless this problem is abated, our society will not produce the quality leaders and responsible public necessary for its continued prosperity.

The problem of disunity within Christianity and among other religions is also serious. Rev. Moon believes that of all people, religious people have the greatest responsibility to help God save America and the other countries of the world. But today, as throughout history, religions and denominations which have professed the same God and even sometimes the same teachings have found themselves persecuting and warring with each other. While some churches have attempted to develop an ecumenical movement, it has largely been a movement among the liberal mainline churches and has therefore failed to address the deepest splits in American Christianity. These are the divisions between liberals and Evangelicals or fundamentalists and between black and white churches. Intolerance, bigotry, and religious arrogance remain deep-seated attitudes in many people. We as Christians ought to realize that God is beyond denomination and doctrine, and that his purpose is to save the entire world, not merely a certain race, nation, or religious group. Jesus prayed that all Christians may become one, and we cannot properly represent God to nonbelievers if we fight among ourselves.

The third problem is the expansion and influence of atheistic communism. This problem can partially be solved by solving the first two problems which I have just mentioned. The denial of God and God's goodness in the world has partially come about because of the failure of the religious community to demonstrate that they have a superior ideal which can abolish prejudice and greed and lead to true, international peace with justice. We speak out against communism and critique its errors because it continues to mislead many idealistic people into a movement which, in the name of peace and justice, has brought untold suffering to humanity and to God. But then we must demonstrate that our alternative will offer better solutions to the injustices which atheistic communism has properly opposed.

Although in prison Rev. Moon could easily be complaining about his unjust sentence, these concerns for the future of America and Christianity have been at the center of his talks to those who visit him and his sermons to church leaders while on Christmas and Easter furloughs. Because Rev. Moon's precise words from prison are only preserved in rough notes, this volume is based upon representative selections from his sermons and speeches which express the same content as what he is now sharing behind prison walls. To share these concerns with a larger audience, Rev. Moon has asked me to publish this compilation of his speeches as a second message from prison.

A word now on how to approach this material. Rev. Moon is an exuberant speaker. His talks are spiced with rhetorical questions, and he has a great deal of give and take with his audience, sometimes sharing delightful humor, other times challenging them to profound seriousness and repentance. Therefore, proper comprehension of these words, removed from their source as they are by an interpreter, several editors, and an absence of the setting and its atmosphere, requires something special. Rev. Moon refers to that something often throughout his talks which are printed here. That something is a pure and open heart and a discerning mind, guided by sincere prayer.

I would like to express my thanks to Dr. Andrew Wilson, who edited this book, and to all those who assisted in the considerable task of its rapid production and distribution. May God grant you the inspiration in reading and reflecting upon this book that He has granted us in its preparation.

New York City   Rev. Chung Hwan Kwak
June, 1985

1
FOR GOD SO
LOVES THE WORLD

Some Christians today may be puzzled when they hear about indemnity and man's portion of responsibility. They think, Almighty God is a God of love with a soft heart. They might think that they can simply believe in Jesus and they will be saved, without having to do anything else.

Let us examine what is meant by "belief in Jesus." To what extent does someone believe in Jesus? Does a person believe in Jesus only as he relates to him as an individual, or Jesus within the family, or Jesus as he reigns over the society, nation, the universe, or the Jesus who is in God? That makes a lot of difference.

A favorite Bible verse of Christians today is John 3:16, which says, "For God so loved the world that He gave His only begotten Son, that whosoever believeth in him shall not perish but shall have eternal life." Many Christians put the greatest emphasis upon the second part of the verse and forget the most important thing: that God so loved the world. God did not love the church, or the individual so much that he sent his only begotten Son. It was because God so loved the world, the universe.

Thus Jesus is the one who came to save the world. When we believe in Jesus the world is very much in our minds. God is in Jesus and Jesus is in God.

Jesus Calls Us to Separate from Satan and Sin

When you say you believe in Jesus, do you only believe in those things which make you feel good? Do you reject those things about Jesus which make you feel painful? We should accept what Jesus taught and do those things which Jesus himself would want us to do. We must not take part in things which Jesus would not like. What are those things which Jesus would not like? They are, simply, Satan and sin.

We are to separate ourselves from Satan and sin and believe in Jesus from that position, rather than from a position in which sin, Satan, and Jesus are all mixed together in our lives. Jesus wants to rule over a world from which Satan and sin are eradicated, not a world in which sin is mixed together with everything and in which people have just a vague belief in Jesus. This is why Jesus said, "Repent, for the Kingdom of Heaven is at hand." For what should we repent? We must repent of the fact that we have been living together with Satan and sin throughout our lives. Then we can serve heaven.

Where are the faithful believers in Jesus and where are the righteous churches that can publicly proclaim proudly that they are absolutely separated from Satan and sin and that they are following Jesus exactly as he would have them do? Since no one can say they are living in perfect love in an ideal world with no suffering and tears, Christians who truly follow Jesus must be struggling to separate from sin and to love the world from the perspective of Jesus, the Savior who labors still to bring the world to God.

But sadly, we know that Satan exists within the churches as everywhere else; there is almost as much sin there as in the rest of the world. All too many Christian leaders are so compromised with the world that what they love and hate is no different from what the rest of the world loves and hates; there is very little difference between the world and those churches. Which would Satan find more pleasure in — the church or the world? Why would he like the sins of the church more than those of society in general? Satan likes the sins of the church more because then he can protest to God, "Look at those people in the church — they don't love others; they even hate others! They are not faithful, either. This must be my church."

The churches which remain this way must perish at the time of the last days along with the evils of the secular world. God has promised that he will destroy all evil at the time of the last days. God would even destroy such churches before the rest of society.

What really surprised me when I first came to America was the way Americans used the names of Jesus Christ and God as an exclamation — not to praise them, but to put them in the worst position. I wondered what people meant when they said, "Jesus Christ!" and I realized that they were describing something bad. What led to this kind of custom? What do the best words imaginable have to do with the worst things that can happen to people? Have you sometimes observed that certain Christians may be worse than people of the secular world? Those who claim they believe in God may actually be worse than those who don't — they are more egoistic, less loving and giving, etc.

This American nation is founded upon Judeo-Christian principles, yet Americans have become very individualistic. Was Jesus an individualistic person? How did Americans come to be so egoistic and individualistic when Jesus had nothing of an egoistic nature? We can come to the simple conclusion that if people really believed in Jesus they would not have become like that. Instead of believing in Jesus for Jesus' sake and for God's sake, some people believe in him for their own benefit. In other words, they use Jesus and God for their own sake. What do you think about this?

Belief in Jesus Brings with it Responsibility to Love the World

Returning to our original point, God sent Jesus to humankind because He loved this world so much. Did humankind believe in Jesus the way God wanted them to, or did people generally believe according to their own discretion and desire? This is the most important determining factor of a person's belief.

The greatest error occurs when people think that they can "just believe" in God and Jesus and they will receive more and more blessings from God. Such people feel they can have everything they want, without doing anything in return. That is similar to the attitude of a thief, who just takes things without working.

Did Jesus believe in God in that way? Did he think that because God sent him as his only begotten son it meant he had all power? Did he feel that all he had to do was to keep on believing and claiming his faith in God, and then he could subjugate all the Roman Empire automatically? If Jesus couldn't do that, what is the justification for thinking that other people can do that? In other words, many people say that Jesus couldn't just believe in God and do nothing, but that we can. Jesus believed in God and we believe in Jesus. Jesus didn't just say, "God, I believe in You so You must bring all the people and all the Roman Empire under my domain." It is clear that such a thing would not work for Jesus. If everything could have come to Jesus automatically, why did Jesus witness? Why did Jesus gather and train the 12 apostles, the 70 disciples, the 120 elders? Why did he have to do all that and endure so much persecution along the way? Jesus went the way of persecution and bloodshed according to God's dispensation; he had no other way to go. Jesus knew the suffering that lay ahead of him, but he also knew he had to go that way in order to accomplish God's will.

Do you think I am placing unnecessary stress on this or do you understand that this point is the most crucial one of belief? Jesus had to go the way he did because he knew what God wanted him to do — namely, to save the world and all mankind by loving them. Therefore, it stands to reason that everyone else who loves Jesus must also do God's will — to love the people of the world and save them.

Because God so loved the world He sent his only-begotten son. Jesus had the obligation, the mission, to make the world one which could receive the love of God. Jesus looked around and saw that the world was not lovable. Is the world lovable today? At this time, there are many different churches with great power and influence in the world. They embrace this world in their own ways. Can God look at them and be completely pleased with them? Communists have even infiltrated the churches and developed theologies to suit their own purposes, such as liberation theology. How can God love such churches?

We can understand that the true, correct faith is not the way many Christians have been going, but rather it is the way Jesus tried to establish in his time — to gather the people, teach the people, and establish the kind of world which God could freely love. Jesus had to love the world in order to accomplish his mission. This was the work of God and also the work of Jesus — it was the purpose for which God sent Jesus. Jesus had to bring the world to God for God to accomplish His purpose of sending Jesus to the world.

Then what would have happened? When all people became worthy of receiving the love of God freely, everything would have been accomplished. God loved the world, so he sent Jesus. When the people of the world are able to freely receive the love of Jesus and God, they will be satisfied. These things have to be accomplished; it is very clear.

The Church Must Confront
the Present World Crisis

Today, God is allowing humankind to be punished through Satan, namely through the spread of communism. This is like a healthy body being invaded by germs —all the cells go on alert, and the white blood cells have to eat up the germs soon enough or else the person will not survive. In this huge, once-healthy country, the germs of Satan and communism are coming in fast. Unless the churches in America come up with the means to eliminate these germs as fast as they spread, the country will not survive.

The "germ" of communism is proclaiming that the society belongs to the working class, the laborers. Satan is claiming this, but God is saying that the world belongs to all God-centered people, not simply to the "laborers." Since Satan has his own movement which is proclaiming an ideology, there should be a movement on God's side which is claiming with an even stronger voice, "No, you are wrong! The world belongs to God-centered, religious people, no matter what economic class they belong to!" The people of the world will be hearing two different voices shouting at the top of their lungs; they will have to make a choice. Which side will have the greater chance of being followed — those who are advocating a false doctrine, or those who are stating a righteous fact?

If groups of Christians emerge from this hopeless world who are loving others, thinking more of serving than being served, and doing as Jesus did, then God will be able to fulfill the promise he made when he sent His only-begotten son. Jesus sacrificed himself and gave up his own life; he remained completely faithful to his mission of making the world lovable by God, making the people worthy of receiving God's love. If some new Christian group emerges at this time, following the path which Jesus trod, then Christianity and the world will have hope for the first time in a long time.

Look around and see which denominations would fit these specifications. What about members of the Unification Church? Why don't we do the same things that many other churches do and believe exactly the same way that they do? Why do we fight against communism? We do this because it is the germ which will destroy all religion if it prevails. Our movement is trampling down on Satan and sin and especially communism, destroying those germs, and on the other hand we are sacrificing ourselves as Jesus did and bearing our own cross so that God can give His love to the world.

Would God say he likes Unification Church members? Would God be ashamed that we work harder than other Christians? No. God would say, "How proud I am of the Moonies!" Are you sure he would say that? How about Jesus? When he looks at the Unification movement, would he say, "Oh, you should be ashamed of yourselves; my other followers don't work the way you do. You embarrass me."? No, instead, Jesus would say, "You are my hope, my pride."

If God loves us and Jesus loves us, what about the people of the world? They might be saying, "We hate those Moonies," but as they say such things, they are watching us, and gradually they are discovering that there is nothing wrong with us. They are gradually coming to like us, and they will come to see hope in us. When other Christians have a real chance to see us and work with us, will they continue to hate us or will they love us?

Jesus sought to bring the entire world to God, and we are determined to do that. Jesus was to confront the Roman Empire. I have been confronting the government of the U.S. and I have pledged to preach the Gospel in Moscow, as well. The most powerful effort of America to stop me has been to put me in jail, but will such a thing stop our movement?

God Does Not Intervene in Human Responsibility

Since God so loves the world, I continue to push you out in order to make this a lovable world. When we undertake something worthwhile, it is important first to have a logical understanding of why we must do it. We do must the things we do because of human responsibility.

Does God really love me or not? When you look at how hard I have worked and how I have been persecuted, don't you think God might have done something more on my behalf? You say that God really loves me, but I might argue with you and say, "If God loves me, what has He ever done for me?" At no time in my entire mission have I ever had a peaceful moment. Wherever I have gone, I was not readily welcomed at first; it was only after I had given much and taught many things that people would begin to understand. I have had to fight continuously to gain ground for God — inch by inch.

If God were to give me the power to work miracles and somehow retaliate against those who persecute us unrighteously and show them dramatically how wrong they are, they would not continue to mistreat us. Why does God allow these unrighteous things to continue? When Jesus was crucified, God was certainly watching the scene. Did God not have the power to stop the Roman soldiers and rescue Jesus from the cross? Jesus was God's own son. What kind of a father could bear to see his own son's blood being shed in such an unrighteous way and not do something? Can we call such a God a God of love and justice? Where was God's justice then? When my court case was over and the judge pronounced my sentence, why didn't God do something? Was it because God did not have the power to do anything? Why did God seem to pretend not to know about it? That is a riddle. In this common yet very important issue comes the understanding of the human portion of responsibility.

Man's portion of responsibility is a cosmic truth. Great discoveries have been made in science, such as Einstein's theory of relativity; however, the discovery of the law of human responsibility is the greatest of all. Without understanding this principle, the most fundamental issues in life remain as a puzzle. "Why do righteous people always have to suffer? Why is a great man's name only resurrected after his death?'' The answers to these questions hinge upon the principle of human responsibility.

The Moonies are the ones who are supposed to appreciate this fact of man's responsibility the most, but ironically you hate it as much as everybody else does. Have you accomplished your portion of responsibility or not? The heaviest consequence of this principle is the requirement that humans make effort to indemnify sin. How long the human indemnity period will last is not known by anyone — not God, not spirit world, not me, not anyone. We may keep asking why the misery in life must go on, but it is a fact that as long as there is sin in the world, we must take responsibility for it. If anybody, including God, were to remove the human burden of indemnity, people could no longer have the dignity of responsible beings. This is not to deny the reality of God's grace, but even grace comes for the purpose of assisting people in fulfilling their portion of responsibility. Therefore God did not intervene when Adam and Eve committed the fall. God did not intervene because he would not violate man's portion of responsibility.

Endure Persecution to Separate from Satan and Find God's Love

I have been persecuted for twelve years in this country, yet I have not done anything evil or wrong. Many people are watching what has been happening to me and are curious about the source of the persecution. Many other well-educated people and scientists can see that even though the majority of the world is accusing Rev. Moon, I have been doing things that are worthy of praise and even assistance.

Yet there is no more efficient way for people to go

from the extreme of being unworthy of God's love to being worthy except by going through persecution. The first thing we must do is separate ourselves from Satan. Do we do that when our lives are cozy and comfortable? No, the best way to separate ourselves from Satan is when we are enduring tremendous persecution. After Satan has opposed someone so much then God can freely love that person, and Satan will have no chance to accuse him any more. Thus, a way is created by which God can more speedily love all those who have been unworthy of his love. Quickly the conditions are made for God to embrace them.

Remember the reason why these things have been happening — everything begins from the point of human responsibility. After man's responsibility is accomplished, what happens then? Once an individual successfully fulfills his portion of responsibility, that person enters the realm of the direct dominion of God. Does God maintain that dominion over a person by giving him a lot of money, or what? It is only through love that God gains direct dominion over mankind. Once that direct dominion is achieved, people can lead the kind of life, for the first time, which God originally intended for them to live.

In the Garden of Eden there was no crime or sin. Adam and Eve could do nothing really wrong except to violate the commandment God gave them. Once Adam and Eve had come under the direct dominion, that would have meant they had passed through the time of the possibility of the fall. The only thing that would have been left for them to do was to experience love. Nothing else would have been truly significant. Love is the most essential and important element of the world; unless someone had violated that, nothing would have been a sin. Therefore all a person must accomplish is to receive the "certificate'' of God's love. God can make the world a totally peaceful place. Satan will be unable to complain against God at all. When we finally possess God's love, we never want to commit a crime or a sin at all. The reason why people commit crimes and sin is that they want something they don't have. When God's love is with us we are satisfied and have no need for anything more.

Since the fall occurred, however, and since restoration efforts have consistently failed, we find that it takes a long and complicated route, step by step, to separate from Satan — from the individual level of indemnity, the family level, the clan, society, national, world level, to the cosmic level.

This is not something I made up; the principle of human responsibility has existed from the very beginning, although it hasn't been so well understood. It existed when Adam and Eve were alive, but all they needed to do was simply keep God's commandment and live for 21 years faithful to God. Before Satan existed, there were no additional indemnity condition to be met. But with the fall and with the multiplication of Adam and Eve's fallen family into a society, nation, and world dominated by Satan, human responsibility became heavier. Now we must separate from Satan on every level by fulfilling conditions of indemnity. This law of indemnity is applicable not just to specific individuals or just to Unification Church members but to everyone. Whether someone understands or believes this law or not, he must eventually go through these steps.

This is the reason why we go the path we go. This is why I have welcomed persecution and will not shrink from the course that lies before me. I never pray to smooth my way or to lighten my burden. I will fulfill my own portion of responsibility.

Do you need restoration by indemnity or not? Do other Christians need it also? What about Jesus — did he walk the path of restoration by indemnity also? Clearly, that was the path he trod. What about Rev. Moon? Yes, no matter what, there is no way I can avoid that. No matter how almighty God is, there is no way even He can avoid the cross of indemnity. He must endure uncertainty and heartbreak as He watches His children stumble along the path. Therefore, we should march on to fulfill our responsibility well.

Love the World as Do God and Jesus

This world is doing such bad things—free sex, with no thoughts of chastity. Many young people today have had so many experiences they feel they are already old and mature. But things are so different within the Unification Church society. Young men have been accustomed to trying to date attractive young women, but that is not the custom in the Unification Church. In the secular world, if a boy gazes at a girl for more than ten minutes he naturally reaches out to kiss her, but here we are together for hours, days, even years and we never kiss! We talk here about love in a different sense. We say we must love the world, love the cosmos, and it is a new concept to young people. A young person might ask himself, ''When does my own love come to me?'' However, he trusts that it will come, so he doesn't have to worry. Is this something good or something bad?

Unheard-of events are happening now. Parents are kidnapping their own children — grown-up children 30 years old and older, college graduates, and so forth. When those children are kidnapped, do they tell their parents, ''Oh, I have been waiting for you to come and rescue me. The church wouldn't let go of me.' "? Or do they look desperately for a chance to escape from the kidnappers and come right back to the church?

Since you joined this church I have always taught you to love your parents; I have never taught you to look at them as ''false parents'' or to denounce them in any way. However, many parents have kidnapped their children and have said many bad things against me. When that happens the children are moved to say, ''On what grounds can you say such things? Have you investigated those charges on your own?'' However, all their negativity is usually based upon the words of other people — ''They said...'' is the only foundation for their negativity. Satan always makes up stories and can inspire people to say anything to suit their own purposes. The world is a deceitful place.

For whom do we go through these things? As we said in the beginning, ''For God so loved the world...'' and because God loves the world so much, we do what we do. God so loved the world that He gave them His only-begotten son — He loves the world, but He cannot give His pure love to the world directly. Therefore, He had to send His son to prepare the world. What kind of love are we talking about, then? God loves the world as a father loves his son; no closer love exists than that between father and son. We are doing exactly this: we are making this a world which can be lovable to God. We are turning the hearts of the children to the parents and ultimately to God.

Jesus completely occupied the love of God, but He did not want to stop there. He knew why God sent him to the world, so he did everything possible to pass along God's love to other people. Jesus received the purest love from God, and he wanted to spread out that love to the whole world. He wanted to make all humankind into God's sons and daughters.

Jesus wanted all the people of the world to be loved by God, just as he was. Jesus was the one who was first-loved by God; all humankind was supposed to be those who were second-loved by God. Therefore, the relationship between Jesus and all humanity is like that between brothers and sisters. How close you can feel to Jesus when you realize that he is your elder brother!

Many Christians have believed that Jesus or God are the subjects of religion and we are their objects and that subject and object can never get close to each other. They are so high and omnipotent that we can't even think about being on the same level of relationship with them; if we do, that is blasphemy. But we can see that Jesus is not the distant subject of religious belief. He is a part of your daily life, just like brothers and sisters in a family, not like the teacher of a religion relating to his followers. Maybe the first step of relationship had to be distant like that, but eventually Jesus wanted everybody to be a part of the same family.

When Jesus is able to approve of the situation on the earth, God can automatically approve of it. When Jesus can love the people, so can God. All he will have to say is, "Father, they are ready to receive your love, so please love them." Thus, the meaning of John 3:16 will be accomplished: "God so loved the world...".

That is the kind of church we are working in and that is the goal we are working toward. We must understand that clearly. The democratic world may decline one day; the communist world will certainly be eliminated and leave no trace behind. However, the love of God will remain for eternity.

God's Hope for America as a
Model of One World Family

Remember, the *world* is God's goal. And just as Jesus willingly gave his life so that the world might live, God wanted all Christians to be willing to give themselves for the salvation of the world. However, today, most Christians are not even close to realizing this heart of God.

God seeks to build one family of humankind. Therefore, the family, church, and nation which God desires transcend all barriers of race and nationality. The people who are a unified blending of all colors of skin, and who transcend race and nationality, are most beautiful in the sight of God and most pleasing to Him.

America is such a microcosm of the world. Transcending nationality and race, God meant America to be a model for the ideal world. Look at your own families. Most families have the virtue of a distinct international character. If your lineage has been in America for some time, it probably unites many different nationalities. In your bloodstream many kinds of blood are blended together. Nations who used to be enemies have united in your blood. When the individuals and families that transcend racial and national barriers gather together to create a church, a society, and a nation, that nation can become God's ideal nation for all peoples.

America is now a big, established country with many customs and traditions. However, the only ones worth following are those which are based upon universal principles. There were two kinds of people among your forefathers. One kind came to this land seeking wealth. The others came to this land seeking God and freedom; they dreamed of building a new nation centered upon God. If the former had become the mainstream of America, there would have been far greater strife, division and struggle between the different races and national groups. The United States would have been filled with unrighteousness and injustice. From the beginning, however, God intervened. Therefore, of all the immigrants, the righteous men of God were to find their proper place as leaders in America. All the different races and nationalities of the world harmonized upon this land. The beautiful tradition of America was set by your forefathers in accordance with God's providence.

God abundantly blessed America, but blessing never comes alone; it comes with responsibility. If a nation forsakes its responsibility, it also forsakes God's blessing. Inevitably the blessing of God will leave, and the nation will decline. Is it not true that the signs of such decline are already apparent in America today?

In the early 1960s, America seemed to be the hope of the world, and the symbol of America was the city of New York. Today, however, the world has lost faith in America, and New York has become a jungle of immorality and depravity. It has been transformed into a city under the attack of evil. Chicago is no different, or Los Angeles. Throughout all of America, Satan is becoming the master. God has been forgotten in this country, and if forgotten, God can only leave America. Now is the very moment that this is taking place!

The time has come for us to repent. Who are the true Americans? True Americans are those who have a universal mind. True Americans are those who believe in the one family of man, transcendent of color and nationality as willed by God. True Americans are those who are proud of such international families and churches and of the nation which consists of all peoples. In the sight of God, there is no black; there is no white; there is no yellow. We should look at the human race as God sees it. America should return to the true founding spirit of the nation, to the ideals which her ancestors sought to establish with sweat and blood. America should return to *Godism*, an absolutely God-centered ideology.

If America wants to keep the blessing of God as the leading nation of the world, she must form a partnership with god. America was born through the providence of God. If she is centered upon God, she will remain united and enjoy prosperity. However, as soon as she turns away from God, she will be divided. God is the cement. With God, America will stay together like concrete. But if God leaves, she will be like sand. When the flood comes, all will be washed away.

When the unifying force of God leaves America, nothing will be able to hold America together. The family will break down; churches will divide, and America will become mortally ill because the cells of her body are decaying. This will be the perfect opportunity for the evil of communism to overtake America. This state of emergency is here now. Someone must do something!

Rev. Moon Comes as a Doctor to Cure a Sick America

There are critics who say, "Why has Rev. Moon, a Korean preacher, come to America? This country is none of his business." If there is an illness in your home, do you not need a doctor from outside? If your home catches fire, do you not need firefighters from outside? God has sent me to America in the role of a doctor, in the role of a firefighter. That is why I have come to America.

Good medicine may taste bitter, and an operation may involve some pain, but the treatment must begin at once. Should a patient complain and push away the doctor's hand when he touches the infected part?

With my entire heart and soul I have been teaching American youth a new revelation from God. They now have a clear concept of what the God-centered family, church, and nation should be like. They also know the dark reality of America. Thus they have become determined fighters to bring new life and salvation to America before it is too late. They know the critical state of the nation. They know the grieving heart of God. And they are absolutely determined to turn the tide back to God. Their enthusiasm is beautiful to behold.

We must reach a decision which will bring hope to America. Who will tackle this difficult situation? Not everyone understands. If some some righteous Christians take on this responsibility for God, maybe America will survive. Can you, who know about it, take on that responsibility?

There are so many dens of prostitution, and pornography is rampant. Who is going to put a stop to it? Who is able to do something about crime, homosexuality and lesbianism, alcoholism, and all the social evils here? Those young people who are becoming addicted to drugs are melting their own brains, like butter. They will not live very long, or if they do they will live like vegetables. Their numbers are increasing every year. Drugs are peddled on the city streets in broad daylight. Who in the world is going to put a stop to all this? Where does the trend of free sex originate from? The movies, television, and so on are stimulating it. Who will put a stop to those gambling places which trap people in another form of addiction?

Certainly American Christianity has the responsibility to stop all these evils, but has it actually been capable of doing it? No, it has not been able to prevail over them. I have called for Christians to unite, because only in unity will there be sufficient strength to overcome the corrupt trend of American life. If Christians don't do it, who will? Will the communists do something to stop it? No, they will encourage the acceleration of evil here because they want to destroy America. Present-day Christianity does not have the conviction or moral power to stop communism here, either. Rev. Moon is one of the handful of people who are trying to alert America, "You must protect yourselves from communism or you will be in peril within a few years." Why do I do this? It is because these things are the origin of God's sorrow, the things that stop humanity from becoming better.

Why do you think I matched black and white people in marriage? Do you think I did it for the sake of fame or reputation? Certainly not. We are seeing the first stages of a racial confrontation that is certain to come in the future unless the true religious spirit flourishes. Black and white people will fight against each other and so much blood will be shed. To prevent such an occurrence, I took the responsibility to bring black and white people together in marriage. This is the solution to those racial tensions.

Anyone with a reasonable mind will be able to see that what I have been doing all these years springs from a deep conviction and principle. How can you Americans take this time casually? You have eyes and ears, but do you hear the scream of this world which is on the verge of dying? It is like a giant animal crying out in pain and agony. Your ears must be able to hear that cry.

Satan blinds people to their true condition and convinces them they are happy. To protect the world from further mistreatment by Satan, we must liberate the young people. Otherwise Satan will have the world in his hands, a world like a living corpse.

When a cancer starts, the victim hardly notices it. As it progresses, he notices it only a little bit. However, that person will probably die unless the cancer is stopped. America is in the same situation. I have been telling you Christians that you cannot remain idle or indifferent. You cannot just think about your own life and your own family and going to Heaven eventually. That attitude among conventional Christians is a problem.

Do you love America? Your love for America means nothing unless you take this task seriously. Go out and appeal to the people, tell all of them what is happening to America. This is our mission — to cry out and proclaim the truth. If they absolutely refuse to listen, then they are already buried by their sin. What else can you do? There is nothing else to do but burst into tears. At that point God will listen to your prayers. If you just pray calmly, God will not respond. If you pray while you are being persecuted and working hard, God *will* respond.

It is not important whether I am persecuted or not. I am only concerned with the will of God and the mission God gave me. I am concerned that without knowing the situation, those who oppose me may be opposing God's will. If what I am doing is not the will of God, it will not go too far anyway. If, however, what I am doing is the will of God, then no matter how much some people reject and persecute us and try to block the way, this mission will succeed.

Why has Rev. Moon come to America where he has encountered such tribulation? Am I pursuing my own honor? Is money my goal, or power? No! Never! I came to America because this is the country which God, our Heavenly Father, has chosen. I came to America because I know the heart of God. I know that in spite of America's rebellion against him, God has not abandoned this country. His will is to make America an example of a godly nation that the nations of the world can follow. I know God's will is to save the world, and to do this America should lead the way. This is why I came to America.

America's Test and Destiny

Today, America is undergoing an internal or spiritual test. She is invaded by moral decay and is confused about her national values and purpose. Meanwhile, the God-denying ideology of communism has risen up to undertake an all-out offensive against the free world. Destroying America is the communists' ultimate goal. More than anything else, America will survive this test only if she stands as God's nation.

America needs God. In this test you cannot win without God, Who is the foundation of all truth, and all true ideology. A confrontation is inevitable between the two worlds—the God-affirming world and the God-denying world. Behind the rattling of nuclear armaments and the skirmishes in Central America lies a confrontation of ideology. America cannot win this confrontation by a reliance on her economic or military power alone. Rather, if she stands as a champion of God, exhibiting the harmonious unity of all races and nationalities, America will be able to win ideologically over atheistic communism.

To do this, world Christianity must unite. The church must liberate herself from sectarianism. She must undergo a drastic reform and achieve an ecumenical and an interreligious unity. For this, we need a spiritual revolution, and it has come in the form of a new Christian movement. The Unification movement has been created by God to fulfill that mission. The new ideology which the Unification Church brings is *Godism*, an absolutely God-centered ideology. It has the power to bring Christians of all creeds, and other religions and conscientious people, into unity without insisting on uniformity of belief. It has the power to awaken America, and it has the power to raise the model of the ideal nation of God upon this land.

With that done, the rest of the world will follow America's example and will build the Kingdom of God upon their respective lands. Then we shall all truly become brothers and sisters under one Father, God. This will be a world of love, a world of happiness. Our planet will be one home, and humanity will be one family. God's will, his long-cherished desire from the beginning of time, will finally be fulfilled. This will be the eternal, ideal world of God. Indeed, it will be the Kingdom of God on earth. We will build it with our hands.

This is our supreme mission. It is truly our God-given, sacred mission. God is crying out to the world, and we are His instruments. The world must respond to His call. Listen to God's commandment. Initiate a courageous march towards the Kingdom of God on earth. Whatever the difficulty, let it not stop us. Our march is God's, and it will go on to the end.

Today let us pledge to God Almighty our loyalty and dedication to the fulfillment of this divine mission. In the name of God, let us unite, and together build the Kingdom of God on earth!

2
PUBLIC LIFE

It is very true that the thoughts of people are usually self-centered. From that point of view, people think about their parents, brothers and sisters, nation and world. Everyone wants to have all his circumstances centered upon himself. If that is the case, how can people relate to one another?

Let us take another perspective. Suppose you are working for a certain company. If you do not contribute to the welfare of that company, sooner or later you will probably be fired. The same is true for school life. A person receives his education at school, but that person is also considered a part of the school. The school is not a part of that person. Some people may wish the school existed solely for them; likewise others wish the nation existed solely for them, but that is not the way society works. The individual must become a contributing part of that nation. In the same way, you are a part of the world; the world does not exist solely for you. The principle of the universe says that each individual lives in relationship to all things and must be disciplined to become a part of the larger whole.

We could represent the universe as a big circle with smaller circles within. In the center is a tiny dot representing the individual. It is natural for each individual to want to be at the center of his universe. No other being besides the human has such a desire. Neither monkeys, dogs nor cats ever think of being the center of the universe. What is it that makes humans the "supreme beings" of the animal kingdom? It is simply this point — only humans recognize that they are linked with all other things in existence.

Each person wants to be "on top" or above everything else. This is human nature. Yet paradoxically, when someone wants to follow his whims, regardless of his environment and surroundings, what are the implications? Such a person will isolate himself from all the larger entities of life. America is one country where the word "I" is spoken very often, but that American "I" is frequently detached and private, isolated from all the larger realms of existence.

Thinking more deeply, we have to ask, "How can I fit into this world, nation, society, and still be able to fulfill my own personal ideals and desires?" Everyone has the tendency to do whatever he wants, and to see events occur exactly the way he likes them, but that seldom happens. Once your thinking is totally self-centered, you will find that you will be expelled wherever you go. The school, the factory and the nation will all reject a person with such thinking. God will reject such thinking.

Think about your own spouse. Although he or she feels very close to you, if you try to do everything centered upon yourself, the relationship will become strained. There must be some common ground toward which you can both dedicate yourselves. When you think about all these things, you must conclude that promoting yourself above everything else is a very, very foolish thing to do.

Freedom Is for the Public Benefit

Let us consider what freedom is. Does having freedom mean that you can do everything only according to your own desire? When speaking of freedom, there is one golden, iron-clad rule that can be set: freedom can exist only within the framework of consideration of the freedom of all. Only upon such a public foundation can freedom truly flourish. The individual must recognize the larger entity before himself. You might say, "What kind of freedom is that? I don't like it." But if you don't honor that standard, your freedom will only bring you destruction, chaos and confusion. Today a very mistaken concept of freedom prevails in this society. Living in a free country doesn't mean that people can do whatever feels good, or follow their every impulse. Yet many people have this attitude.

Suppose the human eye decided it wanted to go somewhere else in the body besides the head, for instance on the arm. That would be very strange, but it is actually similar in principle to Western young people trying to cut themselves off from their proper position within all larger levels of existence. Can a person find happiness in such a way? The person who steps outside of his relationship with the family, society, nation and world and tries to set himself up in some private, isolated realm has actually lost everything! No matter how hard he may work, he cannot connect the results with anything other than himself.

However, when a person stands within his proper position at the central point of the universe, all his work and accomplishments are extended and connected with the broadest levels. Such a person simultaneously possesses everything of value within the universe because he is connected with the whole.

Most people move back and forth, into and out of their proper positions. When a person remains somewhere other than his proper position within the universe, the universe will strive to expel him. That position is similar to a tumor within the body, an alien substance in the wrong place. Many people find a solitary, purely individualistic attitude in life very attractive; they believe they have freedom because they are able to direct everything according to their own will. However, all their efforts to succeed and be happy will be repelled by the force of the universe. They will eventually be pushed into a very unhappy position. But when a person stands in his proper position, all his efforts are aided by the force of the universe and his life is naturally smoother and easier.

Consider what is required to be an important leader with many responsibilities. Certainly the most important leader in the United States is the President. Being the most important person, can he get up every morning and follow whatever whims strike him during the day? Does an important person normally go to bed whenever he feels like it? No, the truth is that every minute of an important person's day has to be accounted for. When he is simply eating dinner, someone will want to know where he is and what he is doing.

Can the President tell everyone to just leave him alone and quit following him around? Can the President discriminate among his many responsibilities and choose only the ones he enjoys taking care of? Can he control the time and place where his various responsibilities will demand his attentions? Certainly he cannot do any of those things. When something happens in the middle of the night, the President must be willing to respond to the situation. If he is not, he cannot be the leader of the nation. In this sense, he doesn't have any freedom. Most of the time he simply has no freedom to do as he pleases.

A typical individual in this country has an extraordinary amount of freedom. Many housewives are free to spend their days entirely according to their desires. A housewife is an individual, but she represents her husband and children within the home. If she detaches herself from those other responsibilities, she detaches herself from her true value. Sometimes a crisis might arise in the house just when the mother is ready to go out and do something she enjoys. Is she free at that moment to ignore the needs of her children and go ahead? She may have the freedom, but she would not be right in doing it. She would not be a good person according to universal principles if she indulged her own desires at the expense of the larger entity, her family. Of course, such a self-centered person will probably believe she is good, but she will find herself suffering from the criticism of her husband, her children and other people in the society. They will all convey the message to her that she is bad. What is "bad" in this sense? A bad person, simply speaking, is one who has abandoned his position within the larger scheme of things and thus has lost his connection with everything else. He is someone who once had something which he lost. The housewife in our example would be rejected eventually by her husband and children if she lived by her selfish standard all the time, and she would deserve the label of "bad person."

Love in the family should be public-minded and unselfish. Selfish love says, "You must love me. I'm here to receive love." That kind of love always drags you down like an anchor. In most cases, American women marry because they want their man to love them; they are eager to receive love. That is wrong. You should change your mind now and think, "I want to get married because I want an object to give my fervent love to." No matter how big and strong a man is, he will be melted by love.

Any love that is not public-minded is destructive love. Which should be more important to the couple, their savings account or their love? In some homes there are two savings accounts, one for the husband and one for the wife. When they borrow from each other they even write a receipt! If the son asks for some money, he writes a receipt and pays it back with interest. Is love cheaper than money and a piece of paper? When you are truly in love, a husband and wife are one body. Your whole body can become sacrificial, so a bank account is nothing. When the wife needs money, the husband's money is hers. Likewise, the wife's money is her husband's.

When someone is praised as being good, he will invariably be a person who brings goodness and benefit to other people. When a good person owns or controls many things, other people welcome it because they realize something good will result. However, a bad person is avoided by others, and even when he has a small amount of wealth, other people are not happy to see it. Goodness can go anywhere within the frame of God's universe and be well received, while evil cannot pass or be acceptable anywhere. Are you a good or a bad person? If you are both good and bad, that is actually bad! Why does a parent urge his child to become good? By doing that the parent is wishing the ultimate benefit for the child. By being good the child will be welcomed throughout the universe. Goodness is unchanging and universal, so a person who is recognized as good in Korea will also be known as good in America. Even in Moscow, people will recognize goodness in someone.

Normally a good person is not able to follow his whims. One aspect generally attributed to a bad person is his habit of indulging himself and living only for his own desires. Therefore within the current popular concept of freedom there is more evil than goodness. Many young people are confused about the true nature of freedom. They think simply following one's impulses is freedom and it is good.

Someone might be a great lover of music, so he might feel that whenever the inspiration strikes him, he should be able to sing at the top of his voice. If he indulges his inspiration at four o'clock in the morning, how would that be greeted by others? His neighbors would not be very enthusiastic about such "artistic freedom."

Directly connected with the level of personal freedom is the family level of freedom; next are the higher levels of society, national and world freedom. It sometimes happens that these different levels of freedom are in conflict. The individual's freedom may not coincide with the nation's freedom. The national freedom may not coincide with the world's freedom. If the greatest value is placed upon the freedom of the individual, the family will have to suffer. If the nation's freedom is given highest priority, the order and harmony of the world can be shattered. The freedom of a smaller level can easily damage the freedom of the larger level if the smaller one takes priority at the wrong time.

Now that you have come to understand this principle, you can examine your past experiences. You have probably asserted your right to individual freedom but without an understanding of its effect on the public benefit.

Freedom Respecting the Law of God

Why must the laws of the nation be followed by all the individuals within that nation? The laws are created for the sake of the benefit and stability of the nation as a whole; they are not necessarily designed to accommodate every individual's preferences. In this way the freedom of the nation is protected and the freedom of the individual is subordinated to that larger good.

By the same token, all living beings within the universe must respect and follow the highest laws of the universe. The law of the universe is the law of God.

Which should the individual value more, his own or his family's freedom? Certainly he should cherish his family's freedom above his own. However, an individual may be willing to sacrifice his family's benefit for his own sake, as when a young man goes out dancing and stays out all night while his family is worried and cannot sleep. What kind of freedom is that? Such "freedom" has no right to exist when it violates the peace and well-being of the family. Likewise the family's freedom must serve the nation's freedom. In order for a family to be protected within the country, it must respect and serve that country. This applies all the way up to the universe-level of freedom, which must be subordinated to God's freedom. At what point does God's freedom become established and secure? God Himself has been suffering because of the blindness and ignorance of human beings.

If an individual does not conform to the expectations of his family, the whole family is disturbed. If a certain family follows a decadent way, the entire society will suffer because of it. If one country pits its own benefit against that of the world, the entire world will suffer and be forced to change the direction of that country.

When God looks at His created universe, He sees it trying to enjoy its own freedom without thinking about Him and He suffers because of that. How do you think God will treat an individual who consistently destroys other levels of freedom? Will He pat him on the head and say, "Fine"? No, God will try to set that person straight. He cannot take any joy in that individual's freedom when it ruins larger levels of happiness.

Many individuals and families pray earnestly for their own benefit. Do you think God is inspired to bless self-oriented individuals and families? God might even have the inclination to cause hardship for such people so that they might realize their error. God is not a bad God; whatever He does is always for a good reason, so if He gives hardship to someone it is to ultimately help that person.

What if someone prayed, "God, if you don't give me what I want, I'll just cut off my leg!" God would look at him and feel, "Go ahead and do it, you self-centered child." Consider the white supremacist who prays, "Oh God, bless this world and bring peace to it — by getting rid of all the black people." Will God grant such a prayer? Absolutely not! God would want to punish and correct such a terrible way of thinking.

Can a saint be the kind of person who goes wherever he feels like going and does whatever he feels like doing? No, the saint is just the opposite. He can rarely do what he feels like doing.

Some people in the secular world think that because Rev. Moon is at the top of the Unification Church, he must have the greatest amount of freedom and flexibility to indulge himself! People believe such things because

they have an incorrect understanding of what a leader is
or should be.

The truth is that wherever I go, I feel I must be able
to answer to my family, my church members and everything around me. Even if I want to go and sit on the
grass, I have to wonder, "Am I taking the spot where
a dog wants to sit? Am I possibly destroying an anthill
if I sit here?" I can never stop feeling responsible for
every motion I make, even the movement of my foot.
This is how I have lived my entire life.

The Freedom of God May Conflict with Smaller Levels of Freedom

Why must I live the way I have? What kind of joy and
meaning do you think I have found in life? I live like
this because I have a clear goal: I am living for the sake
of the freedom of the universe and the freedom of God.
That is why I have come into conflict with all the other
levels of freedom and benefit.

A bad person will not like a good person because their
realms of interest and benefit are always at odds. A good
person always pushes for the benefit of the largest level,
ultimately God's benefit, and this always conflicts with
a bad person's willingness to sacrifice the larger purpose
for his own benefit.

I have been teaching and guiding American young
people with all of my energy, and those who have listened
have changed from their former ways. That slight change
happens to contradict the way the vast majority of Americans want to go. For many Americans, the individual
and the family level of benefit are the only things of
value. Now members of the Unification Church are sacrificing those smaller benefits temporarily for the sake

of God and the benefit of the universe. Therefore society has complained loudly and has strongly opposed their changing.

The fact is that in order to establish God's dominion and God's freedom, all the lower levels of freedom which come into conflict with that must be sacrificed. Persecution is an automatic reality whenever someone tries to advance toward God's level of freedom. You may ask, "Why don't you exalt individual, family and every other kind of freedom at the same time you are honoring God's freedom?" However, such a thing is not possible; when all the other levels of freedom are violating God's freedom, one must be subordinated to the other. If the world is going against the direction of God and His freedom, someone must push it toward the proper direction. That is why we are living the way we do and why we receive the kind of persecution we receive. People call us "Moonies" with great scorn now, but at the same time, we are being elevated in the eyes of God and the universe.

Why do we choose to go a difficult way? Actually, we have no other alternative than the way we have been going because the ideal can only be realized in this way. Universal freedom and happiness can only be found when we ensure God's happiness and freedom. Only when the benefit and freedom of the highest Being is assured can all the lower levels of being have their lasting happiness and freedom. Once God's level of freedom and happiness has been achieved, He can bring about true universal peace and happiness for everyone on every level of existence.

This is the conviction that has guided my entire life. In the beginning, no one understood me, but gradually more and more people could appreciate what I was teaching. I have lived as God's ambassador coming into hostile territory; all the forces of "authority" have investigated me, since I am different from others. Although many countries have tried to stop me, and even now the U.S. government has imprisoned me as a criminal, another realm is happy and excited. All of Heaven is eager to assist me because they understand that I am working to establish and maintain God's freedom, the highest level of goodness. If God himself were here on earth, He would certainly have been arrested, put on trial and jailed, but once He was able to gain freedom, He would be able to create the Kingdom of Heaven on earth. At that point God could live happily with His people within a truly happy, free world.

When the court asked me to come and be present, did I have the freedom not to report? Did I have the freedom to avoid jail? No, now Rev. Moon has the freedom to be persecuted. Is that the kind of freedom I desire? No, it is painful and bitter many times, but I persevere through all these experiences, conquering them in order to acquire true freedom, true joy, and true fulfillment. Whenever there is conflict between two elements, the more public element will ultimately prevail, be victorious, and move on. The universal principle is such that the one who has the most public standard will be triumphant. The one with the less public standard will diminish.

Churches Should Be Training Grounds
for Public Life

As a Christian, how public is your standard? Let's each grade our church's public standard. If you are really convinced that your church's public standard is the highest possible one, then hold on to your commitment and persevere. For whose sake should you do that? It is not just for your sake, but for the well-being of the public. If you are truly moving forward unselfishly for the attainment of that public goal, God will always be following you and aiding you.

We aspire to be number one in living for the highest purpose. In the Olympic games there are many kinds of competitions, but the contest which has the most prestige is certainly the marathon race. It is the supreme test of the human spirit and body; nothing else requires more endurance and strength. Once a person wins the gold medal for the marathon, he is admired by everyone else. Likewise, in the competition of living the highest public life everyone would like to win the gold medal. Since the goal is high, and since a public life runs so contrary to the prevailing American system, an incredible amount of hardship must be overcome to achieve it.

Sometimes people cheat in order to try to win in an easy way. Even though a person ran 26 miles in a marathon, if he were to cheat by riding piggyback for just ten meters, he would lose the honor of winning. Even if someone rode piggyback for five meters, then got off and retreated ten meters and started running again, such a thing could not be accepted, because the rules of the race were violated. In other words, because the desire to cheat was there, the honor was lost. You cannot violate the rules of the race or the rules of the universe and be a winner.

Our goal of living as Christians is to comfort the heart of God and to create the world of which God and Jesus will approve. Can we go an easy way to reach that goal, or randomly do whatever we want to do? Rev. Moon is the coach in the Unification Church's marathon race toward that goal. Should he give the runners an easy training schedule, or should he push them every minute of the day so that they can accomplish the goal? Which kind of coach is best?

The Unification Church is under a tough coach, that's for sure! After the members have received two or three year's discipline from this coach, they cannot help but change. People recognize these changes. They see that under Rev. Moon's tough coaching they become very charming and attractive, and they say, "I wish I could have a son-in-law like that!" People say all kinds of bad things about Moonies until they actually meet one of them. First they may think that he or she is the only good one; but then they meet another one, then another, and another, one after another! When they realize that all of them are such good people, they completely change their opinion.

What about you Christian ministers? Do you give easy approval to anything your members may do, even when their motives are self-centered, or do you labor day and night to educate them and lift them to a consciousness of the public good? Maybe some in your congregation will rebel and refuse your discipline. You should teach them to choose the public way of life as the best way to ultimate happiness and fellowship with Christ. The person who only lives according to his own selfish desires is simply digging his own grave.

We Are Born for a Public Purpose

True victory can only be attained by a person with a public heart doing public deeds. The word "public" is synonymous with "unselfish." We have come to understand why we have to pursue this public way of life, even under persecution. People just don't understand why there are still thousands of young people following me even though I have been jailed by the U.S. government. In our public path, prison is just one more obstacle we may have to overcome. Can you determine that you can live your entire life for the sake of righteousness and the public value, always overcoming the obstacles and attacks against you?

Sometimes you start to think more pragmatically, looking for easier ways to dodge difficulty. You might look at it another way, thinking that a little while later you will try to achieve the ultimate goal, but for now you will just do anything you want to do. I thought about those shortcuts a long time ago, and I came to the conclusion that there is no easy way out. We must each think, "I was born for the public purpose, so I am going to walk the public path every inch of the way."

Do you think that my parents decided that they had to have a son and refused to give birth to a daughter? Can a woman pick in advance the day her child will be born? Is it possible for a child to determine what his character will be? Can a child dictate the love of his parents? No, the love of his parents is almost beyond his control. It is not at your will that you were born, but someone else's will. You were conceived through uncontrollable conditions, your parents' love, and you were shaped by your environment as you grew. Some mysterious power is definitely working in our lives.

Maybe you would rather look like a certain movie star, but you cannot shape your own features. You have to recognize that behind each of us is something larger than ourselves. Where did this brother here get the material to grow from a six-pound baby to a 200-pound man? He is indebted to nature, which freely offered nourishment to him. Is the air you breathe your own possession? Does the sunlight belong to you, or the food you eat? Even your sexual parts come from nature. Nothing really belongs to you; you are only a custodian of these things while they are on loan to you. From the very moment that you were born, nothing was yours. As you grew you became more and more indebted to your parents, to nature, your society, your nation, and so forth. Suppose nature decided to reclaim all the material that it has loaned out to mankind!

Your vegetables will have some opinion about whether or not you are worthy of eating them. In that respect we are all under public scrutiny. In a publicly-oriented universe, how dangerous it is to live only for oneself; it is like sitting on a bomb while striking matches! Of course, you are free to light matches, but the public would indignantly say that you are a saboteur of the public good.

If a selfish person is sitting on a chair, that chair will even have the urge to kick him off! If he stubbornly believes that the chair is his personal property, all the other things around him will see the inside and feel that he doesn't deserve to sit on that chair. A selfish attitude is totally abhorrent to nature. In looking back on your life with all this in mind, you could reasonably feel accused by the things around you for living selfishly in the past. But you can tell them that now you want to change and you want to live a public life.

The motivation behind my ministry in America is to pursue the public good. I have given my heart, soul and resources for the sake of this country, because it is so central to God's providence for the salvation of the world. My public position has been that since America is the center of the free world upon which all smaller nations depend and since America is in peril, it is necessary that other parts of the world support America at this time.

History shall be the real judge of how America has

treated Rev. Moon. Regardless of the present situation, the time will come when a more publicly-minded group of Americans will praise and honor Rev. Moon for what he has been doing. No matter what, we are walking the righteous road every day. We must be strong and bold, because we have nothing to be ashamed of.

God's Heart is the Ultimate Public Level

No one has absolute freedom in his life. We do not decide how long we will live. Everyone lives under this universal rule, whether or not he is great and influential. We never know the moment of our death, so each person should be prepared by living according to the most public standard.

Your family is a higher public level than you as an individual; the society is higher than your family; the nation is higher still; the world is more public than your nation; God is more public than the world, and God's heart is the ultimate realm of public-mindedness. Why is the heart of God the highest standard of public life? There is no other heart or mind that can embrace the entire universe with love.

Someone may ask why he can't just jump in one leap to God's heart, that highest standard of public life. But that is an impossible shortcut. A giant oak tree started many years ago as a tiny acorn, which grew into a small shoot, then a sapling. Could the sapling decide that it would become a big tree overnight? Of course not. When the tree was young, it was vulnerable to many dangers such as drought, and when it became big, it was exposed to other sorts of dangers such as winds and lightning. The tree had to follow the rules of nature in order to become fully grown. In the same sense, there are certain steps for an individual to follow in his life. The individual must learn to live for the sake of his family; the family learns to live for the sake of society; society exists for the sake of the nation; the nation for the sake of the world; and all of these are to find harmony in devoting themselves for the sake of God and God's heart.

Once the individual has reached that highest public level, he finds the greatest personal fulfillment. He can automatically recognize that everything is related to him and feel a part of the universe without even trying. With this kind of existence, you have no contradiction or conflict, but only harmony with your environment. In such a world you can truly say you are free and can enjoy eternal freedom. That is the ultimate goal of our lives. At such a time, you will come to the realization that you are truly the center of the universe, but not because you have promoted yourself into that position. The universe will push you into that position because it will be proper for you to be there.

Within the minds of people there is a glimmer of understanding that we were destined for that central position in the universe, yet too often people try to obtain it by denying every other element in the environment. They want to take the shortest path to their goal, trying to gain instant satisfaction. It would be nice if someone could just press a button and automatically see a harmonious, peaceful world, but that is not possible. I started my path sixty years ago and have carried on the struggle all of my life. Even today the struggle and the journey are not complete. I knew that every step along the path would bring me closer to the goal. This is the reason so many have followed me. Certainly there are greater speakers and more comfortable churches, but Unification Church members have given up all these fine things in order to listen to an oriental man who has to use an interpreter. It is because they have discovered here the most public life.

The value of a person is not determined by the kind of work he does. Your motivation, thinking and heart are what determine your value. When your thoughts are 100% for the public purpose, no door will be closed to you. Even a newly-married couple would want to open their home to the person with the most public standard.

Suppose the President of the United States has an appointment to come to your home. What makes it such an honor? The President is not coming as a private individual, but as the head of the nation, in the most public position in the country, that is why it is a great honor for him to visit. The President is in a very public position, but within God's universe, there is an even greater public position. The person who lives for the highest public purpose in God's point of view would certainly be welcomed by everyone in the universe. In this respect, there is no difference between white, black or yellow; everyone, regardless of his race, will feel honored to receive a visit from such a public person. Even hell and heaven are the same in the sense that they will open their doors and wait for him. The most public person can go anywhere, even if there are normally locks and bolts on the doors. In this sense the public person enjoys total freedom.

The Supreme Court of Heaven Vindicates Me

Is the U.S. Supreme Court the highest, ultimate court? No, there is another historical, super, Supreme Court in heaven, where God Himself presides. In that court, God and history have judged that Rev. Moon is not only innocent, he is also honorable. The verdict has already been reached about what kind of public life and standard Rev. Moon has lived.

Most people think courts are found only on earth, but I know that there is a Supreme Court of Heaven. Everyone on earth must face that Supreme Court of Heaven someday. I have no fear; the road of righteousness is always a road for the bold and strong. Do you think it is easy to pass the judgment of God's Supreme Court? I want to see you judged as honorable, and that is why I send you to Africa and South America, to primitive jungles, to suffer for the public purpose with the most public minds. In this respect, our way of life and our value system are supreme; nothing can surpass them.

Normally, when someone has to go to court he feels very bad; certainly he doesn't have a wonderful morning service beforehand! When the indictment against me was handed down, I was out of the country; I didn't have to return, but I immediately flew back to face the charges. My desire was to allow true justice to prevail; therefore, I could not evade national-level laws. I have to go over all obstacles and therefore I confronted these charges face to face. Throughout history, righteous persons have gone the same way. It doesn't matter where I go, even to a prison, for the flag of righteousness shall be unfurled. I never feel lonely; I am with righteous people who have suffered and been persecuted throughout history. The attention of God is always directed to that position of righteousness.

Never make excuses for yourself, no matter what. Walk the path of righteousness with your chin held high; be bold and strong. Even if I should no longer be among you, today's sermon should be a guide for the rest of your life. The spirit of this teaching will live forever, even if Rev. Moon is no longer here. The time will come when righteous people of America will take this path and follow the example of my teaching. Then America will once again be moving in the right direction. I do not focus on those Americans who are opposing me at the present time. I am thinking of those righteous Americans of the future who will follow my path. This is the way I look at America, and there is no doubt that such a thing will happen. My prayer today is for my accusers, that their lives may not become miserable because of the judgment of history. I ask God to forgive them.

You may forget many things, but never forget this one point: we are destined to live a public way of life; we were born for this. Who will be the judge of whether you have lived for the public good? God will be the judge, and His verdict alone will stand throughout history. Each person is creating a public record of his entire life; and it is being recorded for judgment in that ultimate courtroom of Heaven.

In that courtroom, Satan will be your prosecutor, Jesus will be your defense lawyer, and God will be your judge. Everyone will be called into that courtroom eventually. The public way of life is your preparation for the final judgment in God's courtroom and the foundation upon which you will be found "not guilty" and an honorable citizen of the universe. Every deed you do in every moment of the day is recorded and will be judged in that final courtroom. The criterion will be whether or not you lived for the public purpose.

Let us live the public way of life. I want to conclude my sermon today by saying that every one of you who truly follows my teaching will be judged honorable; your public way of life will shine like a beacon of hope for the rest of humanity and for all generations to come. I want you to be those beacons of hope and light.

God bless you. Amen.

3
LOVE AND THE PURPOSE OF LIFE

If you asked God, "What pleases You the most?" how would He respond? Would He say, "I like diamond rings the most!"? No, God has no need for any such thing. But God created humankind for a reason. Why were we necessary? God needed to create humankind in order to fulfill His love. It is for the sake of love that human beings are the supreme creations. God's love is the original giving love; it is the unselfish, *agape* love.

We need food, shelter, clothing, knowledge, power, money and so on, but our foremost need is for love. Isn't that true? Are the love of God and the love of people essentially different things? They are the same thing in essence, but God's love is subjective, unselfish, giving love and humanity's love is an objective, receiving love.

Human nature causes men and women to desire certain relationships of love. It is very logical and natural for the members of any unit, for example a family, to desire to receive the love and attention of the head of that unit. Thus children desire the love of their parents. On the level of the nation, the citizens want to be cared for by their leader, their president or queen. Is that a natural desire of only white people, or do black and yellow people have the same desire? We can see that the craving for love is a universal desire, regardless of race, nationality or culture.

People like to talk about equality, but there is really no true equality in society because everyone is different and on different levels. But there is at least one fundamental point of equality with which every human being is endowed, and that is the capacity to receive love, specifically the love of God. In this respect, all people are equal.

The most important thing for both God and humankind is love. When there is equality in love, there is equality in everything. There is a definite relationship between the two loves. Why is God trying to save humankind? Why can't He just forget about us or even destroy us? God lost His first relationship of love with Adam and Eve because of the human fall. Adam and Eve were not only the recipients of the first love of God, but they were also created as His very own son and daughter. Therefore, God can never abandon them, even through His love was lost through them. Their redemption became God's goal.

God and the Ideal of Marital Love

When God sees His son and daughter, do you think He would have an intense craving to be with them and dwell within them? What about men and women? Knowing that God's love is foremost and supreme, don't you also want to be totally bound with that love? God wants to enter into His children and the children want to enter into God.

It is natural that men and women would instinctively know how to welcome the love of God within themselves. You would never want to lock yourself out from the love of God. In fact, you would want to open yourself totally and without a shred of reservation to receive it. Let's say you have a certain secret territory within you. When the love of God approaches, would you want to maintain that secret place? Would you not want to open every secret place to Him?

God wants to dwell inside His children, within their most sacred and holy places. He doesn't want to stay on the surface or anyplace else. There is no place that the love of God cannot penetrate. It can enter your eyes, nose, mouth, and all of a sudden you feel such an incredible sensation. God's love can penetrate every single cell of your body.

Human bodies are composed of cells, and it is the inherent nature of those cells to enjoy and desire love. You have a physical body which you can touch and also a spiritual body, which you cannot touch. But that spiritual body is the subject. Your whole system, body as well as spirit, is constructed so that it craves love. When your body and your spirit become perfectly united, you cannot avoid being approached and entered by true love. True love is like the welding agent which binds your body and spirit together.

When people are in their teen years, they are getting ready for love. Teenagers are very romantic; they are usually intense poets. That is the sign that they are opening up to the fullest sensations of love—body, mind, and spirit. They are saying, "I am ready to receive you, love. Please come into me." There should never have been a fall; thus every experience of love would have been Heavenly and joyful. The problem is that those teen years became a time of satanic love, not God's love.

Your eyes are in the position to oversee everything, and thus they are symbolic of God. When a baby is conceived, its eyes are the first things to develop. Within the eyeball, the white part represents your physical body; the iris represents your spiritual body; and the pupil, the black dot in the center, represents God. Actually, the eye is a beautiful example of how a person should live. Centered upon God, we have a spiritual body and then a physical body. The opening in the center could be called God's love dot. When God looks somewhere, the spiritual and physical bodies also look there. In other words, God's direction is identical with the direction of the spiritual and physical bodies.

Both men and women should have their eyes of God's love. When they looked somewhere, where would they normally look? Would a woman's eyes look primarily at the animals and the trees? No, she would naturally be attracted to look at a man, even if he were ugly or clumsy. The form of a man is attractive to a woman's eyes. How about a man's eyes? He is not primarily interested in the plants or the blue skies. He is interested in looking at the curves of a woman! Electricity builds up between a man and a woman; God would generate more and more voltage between them. Finally, quivering with thousands of volts, they would unite together in a tremendous explosion, creating a huge fireball.

When they are surrounded by that fireball of love, are only the man and woman within, or is God also included inside? Yes, God is there with them. What would God feel? He wouldn't say, "I'm just bored." He would say, "I'm satisfied now!" When God is totally satisfied, he is intoxicated. In love, you can be molded into any form or shape, like bread dough. God, too, will be completely pliable. That dough will have God at its core.

That is the ideal of creation which God longed to see. God's ideal of creation is fulfilled in the relationship between perfected, unfallen men and women, in their love centered upon God. That is the way in which men and women intermingle with God. Love was designed to be the most glorious, supreme and beautiful thing, but because of the human fall, love became the dirtiest, most corrupt and degraded thing.

Where do the mind and body come together in unity? Human beings are polarized into plus and minus, men and women. In electrical wiring, you need plus and minus parts fitted together to create a circuit. Men and women have their own unique sexual organs where every nerve system is concentrated. Those are the most important organs. If they are used properly, that is good; but if they are misused, that is very wrong. The man's love organ is located at the center of his body, as is the woman's. These organs are ultimately connected to their power stations, which is God. When plus and minus meet together, there is a circuit and the power flows. When they meet, they produce a spark; that spark signifies unity and also creativity.

When that spark occurs between men and women, a magnetic field of love is created. In that spark, the entire creation vibrates together with that magnetic field, flowing down from God. Therefore, the entire creation is like a love machine. God created human beings to be the internal part of the machine, while the universe is the external machine. Both vibrate together with the same wave of love.

Women naturally want to protect the most private parts of their bodies, particularly their bosoms. But you don't want to stay covered and hidden throughout your entire life; you want to open that part of yourself at the proper moment of your life. When do you have the desire to open yourself? It is when your true love approaches; then you want to open yourself up. Once you meet with your true love, that is permanent; there can be no alternative love.

The ultimate stimulation and fulfillment of men and women is that of true love; there is nothing greater. That is like the anchor of your life. You do many things, going here and there, but you always remain connected to that central anchor in your life. Once your earthly life is over, you can take that anchor, that stake upon which your whole life was hung, and go to spirit world with it. There you can anchor it into the heart of God. That is the only thing you can take with you to spirit world. Once anchored in the heart of God, husband and wife can feel satisfied and fulfilled.

If there had been no fall, physical love between men and women would always have been the most sacred act. But that most holy place of men and women was taken by Satan and became the most dirty place. In the Temple of Solomon there was a holy place and a most holy place. The most holy place was closed at all times except to special people, the priests and holy men, who could enter for the purpose of prayer and ceremony. By the same token, a husband and wife are supposed to open their most holy places only to each other for the fulfillment of heavenly love. They are never to defile them by allowing a stranger to enter.

When the love of husband and wife is consummated to this most holy degree, God is dwelling with them all the time. In that condition, self-denial is not necessary; one's body and mind are the most holy places. By loving oneself, one loves God. Self-denial became a necessity in religious life because the most holy temple came to be occupied by Satan. Thus, when one loved himself he was also loving Satan. That is why men had to deny themselves to remove Satan from themselves, for the ultimate purpose of putting God within. That is the whole religious process. From the point of view of the ideal of creation, however, every person's body and mind were supposed to be the dwelling places of God.

Love is More Precious than Life

Every man and woman possesses his or her own holy, holy place. Can someone purchase that holy place with money? Even in the secular world, people recognize that love cannot be bought with money. How much more valuable is love in the Heavenly world? A fundamental question is whether life or love is the most precious. You say love, but why? No matter how long you live, your biological existence has no value unless you are experiencing love. Life does not automatically connect us with the most holy place, but love does.

Do you men live for the purpose of eating three meals a day? Or perhaps you only care about sleeping eight hours a night? No, it is for the sake of love that we live. That is how God created us. therefore, Men and women are willing to sacrifice their own lives for the sake of their loved ones. The word "holy" must be connected to love; it is only in the context of love that the word "holy" has meaning. For example, any husband who is able to sacrifice himself for his wife's sake is a holy husband; the reverse is true as well. The person who is willing to die for the sake of his parents is called a child of filial piety; he is a holy son or daughter. The person who gives his life for his nation is considered a holy patriot. Likewise, the person who gives his life for the sake of all humanity is a holy saint.

Love is the supreme value. Therefore, your love is not yours alone, but it exists for the sake of others. All must bow down before love. It is only through love that you can connect yourself to God, the central plus of the universe. Therefore, love has power and dominion over all things.

Equality in Love

With this point of view, how can any man ever be scornful toward the holy body of a woman, whether she is beautiful or ugly? Can the white man claim that love is only white? Or perhaps the yellow people think love is yellow? Human beings are being elevated to the position of recipients of the love of God; in that way, you are gaining your true human dignity. Does love have a particular color? Centering upon God, love truly bestows equality to everyone.

We could compare the value of two people, a pretty woman and a plain woman for example. Suppose the plain woman had more truthfulness and genuineness. We must have a discerning eye, capable of telling the difference between people. We must be able to see when a person has more quality than another, even though that person might be physically less attractive than others. It is true that the woman who has a less beautiful appearance often tends to have more love within her than a woman who is extremely beautiful. Perhaps you men might say, "I would like a good quality woman who is also beautiful!" However, chances are that you cannot have both; it is either/or. There is a Korean adage that says, "There is no truly blessed woman who is beautiful."

When a woman is beautiful in her youth she will often try to maintain her beauty even after it is gone. She may also continue to be boastful and aggressive as she was when she was young and beautiful. When such a woman approaches, people are daunted by her. On the contrary, the woman who is just average-looking will not be obsessed by her looks but will focus upon her internal beauty. Everything is relative — if a woman has one quality, she usually won't have the other and vice versa.

Suppose we had a lump of 24-carat gold and a sculpture of George Washington, also made of 24-carat gold. The lump is very rough and dull, as if someone had retrieved it from a trash can. Suppose both items weighed the same, say one pound. Which has more value? In terms of the gold, they both have the same value. But then let's say that the sculpture was only 18-carat. Which would be worth more money then? It would be the ugly lump because it was pure gold. We are not so much concerned about how gold looks or what shape it is in, but rather about its quality and whether it is truly 24-carat or not.

Similarly, there are all kinds of people — different shapes, sizes, colorings, different types of character and personality, and so forth. However, the most important quality of any person is his or her truthfulness. The value of a person is determined by how genuine he or she is.

Above all your other qualities, your true love must be genuine. Thus you must look at people and things with your eyes tuned in to true love. Do you look at your spouse with the eyes of genuine love? What percentage of your life do you see your spouse through the eyes of true love? Perhaps only 50% of the time? Or maybe only 10% of the time? You can evaluate yourself — if you only look at your spouse with eyes of true love 10% of the time, then you can know that you are 90% impure. You know you have to change if you have that much impurity. Ask yourself seriously how pure you are.

The Corruption of Secular Love

The ideal of love within the Unification Church is truly magnificent in its beauty and dignity. Viewed from the Unification concept of love, the American standard of love is impossible. For example, a man might have a relationship with different women every day, or even more than one. The most beautiful women often feel that men are their servants; they think they can maintain relationships with dozens of men, night after night. Many people have the attitude that love is something that is just for fun. But those people are the worst criminals in the sight of God; they are defiling the most holy places of other men and women.

According to the Old Testament, when someone full of sin and corruption tried to enter the most holy place of the temple he would be punished immediately by God with instant death. By the same token, if someone within our society transgresses against another person's most holy place, knowingly or unknowingly, the entire universe will inevitably punish him or her.

Looking at the secular society from this viewpoint, we can see incredible evils and immorality happening everywhere. There is so much to be cleaned up. I want you to understand that the human fall wrought total destruction upon God's dream of love and degraded the most holy experiences into the most shameful. The original love was supposed to be men's and women's ticket into Heaven; but on the contrary they purchased tickets to Hell through illicit love. We must cleanse the love of the world and stop the multiplication of the consequences of the human fall.

Because of the human fall, human beings must stand in shame before the lowest forms of creation. The supreme creation of God was degraded to a point far below that of the animals, plants and minerals. Americans today think that they can continue to pursue a degraded form of love and enjoy greater and greater prosperity, but that is not the case. From God's point of view, the way of life in secular America today deserves a worse judgment than fire and brimstone.

It was because of an illicit relationship of love that the fall occurred. We can say that the last days predicted by the Bible will be the time when selfish, individualistic love reaches its perfection. When we see that most people are living solely for themselves, that must be the last days, because that is the perfection stage of the fallen act. In such a world, anything other than individualistic love is scorned. There is no room for the love of the country, love of humanity, and certainly no room for the love of God.

Such a trend began in the adult world but it has now come down to the realm of teenagers. That is why we have the so-called "me generation." You can see that this is happening in today's society; thus you know that we have come to the end of this world. There is virtually no way of controlling the promiscuous immorality of many of today's young people. Parents cannot control them, teachers are powerless, and society cannot do anything, either. American society has degenerated to such an extent that it is making Sodom and Gomorrah look trivial. The "gay liberation" movement is gaining tremendous momentum, but that is a tool of Satan by which he seeks to destroy the most precious, fundamental values of God. The gay movement seeks to justify itself through gaining legal, political and ultimately moral power, but this is disgusting in the sight of God.

When you are stimulated by love, particularly first love, it is an overwhelming experience. When you are in love you talk all night and still are not bored. You are temporarily blinded and can't think of anything else. For the sake of that love you would willingly sacrifice yourself. That is noble love. But today's Americans don't even think about finding a true love for which they could sacrifice. If they want to find out whether the other person truly loves them or not, they face a dilemma. Men and women come together just for convenience or fun, and there is no true love there, so even after several years a person cannot really know if the other person loves him.

Are there any children who like to see their parents get divorced? Does anyone get married with the knowledge that he will get a divorce in the near future? Why does divorce come unexpectedly and against their will? In many cases divorce comes because of another love affair. Because there was no concrete love in the first place, the foundation of love easily breaks apart.

Divorce has even become a business in this country and good-looking young women go into a marriage for some strategic purpose. They find a rich man, marry him, and then get divorced in order to get a chunk of his money. Increasingly the custody of a husband's money and his wife's money is a secret they keep from each other. If they revealed everything then the other person might want a divorce to get part of it!

Today's American young people look for nothing but fun and self-satisfaction, and they are blind to anything else. Their parents even encourage this fallen culture. When they see that their teenagers don't have girlfriends or boyfriends, they get worried and tell them to go out with several people and pick one they like. Is such education advocated in the Bible? Would any righteous religion teach such a principle? That kind of habit is part of a doomsday culture and it deserves judgment. America is totally blinded and becoming more aimless every day.

If America keeps going in its present direction, the time will come when the rest of the world will abhor America. A man with any conscience could never tolerate what America is doing today. What is the so-called glamorous life being led by Hollywood stars? They are basically self-centered. Are their love affairs pure and upright? I feel such a strong urge to reach out and clean up the kinds of things that happen in places like Hollywood.

If any nation or community lives a dog-like life, it is bound to decline because God's principles are uncompromising. In the Bible it is recorded that Sodom and Gomorrah were judged by brimstone and fire because dog-like people lived there. They were totally immersed in a sensual life and interested only in satisfying their physical appetites. God could not tolerate such people, who were totally destroying their love. The Roman Empire was once mighty, yet it collapsed, not from outside force but from within. From the emperors down to the everyday people, everyone was pursuing a sensual life. Some of you may have visited Pompeii in Italy, which was destroyed by a volcano. Archeologists have uncovered evidence by which they can reconstruct life at the moment the volcano erupted and covered the city, and it was truly dirty and lustful, totally morally corrupt.

We Must Follow a Religious Life to Purify Love

Someone has to step forward to clean this mess up. But human effort alone cannot do such a task. God must intervene in a religious, spiritual way. The satanic phenomena in the world are not totally of man's making, but Satan's. The American public, particularly the young people, have become Satan's victims. What churches in America represent God's will and are trying to clean up the mess? God wants to liquidate the entire immoral and evil tradition of love in the world and He needs champions to accomplish this. Among the foremost of His champions are the members and families of the Unification Church, led by Rev. Moon.

As husbands and wives, you hold the keys to each other's holy places of love; only you can open up those places, no one else. That is the proper understanding of the husband and wife relationship.

You must be able to discipline yourselves. You cannot just use your holy place at whim. That holy place must be kept pure. In this way, the corrupt and immoral world will be cleaned up. This is the place where Heaven and hell can be determined.

The human fall did not occur from just eating some kind of physical fruit from a physical tree called The Tree of the Knowledge of Good and Evil. God asked men and women to grow into the perfection of pure love but they did not do that. The children of God united in illicit love with the servant of God, the archangel; that was the fall. They were polluted with a satanic love whose motive and content was selfishness and rebellion against God. Because of the fall, a selfish and sinful love came to replace God's love in the first human family and has been propagated from generation to generation. The Heavenly lineage of God was lost; we say that the bloodstream of man was stained and it has to be "cleansed." For that reason, bloodshed became inevitable in human history. When stained, satanic love is coursing through the human body, there is no way for the pure love of God to come and dwell there.

How can you cleanse your stained blood? You have to die to yourself first and be reborn as new men and women. This explains the paradoxical nature of much of the Bible's teachings. This is why Jesus told his disciples, "Those who seek to gain their lives will lose them, but those who lose their lives for my sake will find them." They were being told that they had to die to themselves.

All of human history has occurred on the foundation of the stained blood lineage. Regardless of how many people there are on the earth — 4 billion or 10 billion — we must return to the root and cleanse it. Then we can begin anew, according to the unstained, purified lineage. Basically, that has been the work of God in history.

Behind every single person on earth today is a long lineage, tracing all the way back to his roots. You have the concept, "I am a white person in America," or whatever, but God is saying that you must eliminate from your mentality the "I am" attitude. You must get rid of whatever self-concept you have now in order to become a new self. A new "I am..." must be given room to be born.

This is the reason religion has always taught self-denial. Regardless of what great work you might do, if you cannot succeed in this requirement you will end up in hell. This is why Jesus said, "If you love your parents or your spouse or your children more than you love me, you are not worthy of me." That is because everyone besides Jesus sprang from the satanic lineage; if people loved them more than they loved the son of God, they could not be worthy to be with him.

Regardless of your position or title, the most important requirement is that you love Christ more than you love anything or anyone else. Otherwise, you are not worthy in the sight of God. We have seen an incredible phenomenon within the Unification Church in the fact that the parents of some of the members have tried to kidnap them. It is very evident that we are loving God above everything and everyone else, so other loved ones sense some reduction in your love. Thus they may feel jealous and try to pull you away.

People in the secular world pursue material and worldly values, such as status and wealth. But the members of the Unification Church are seeking to get out of the fallen realm; they go the reverse direction. In the Unification Church, instead of seeking to wear beautiful clothing and eating delicious gourmet foods, we wear simple clothes and we fast. Secular women wear lots of glamorous makeup, but Unification Church women wear very little makeup.

The highest religious teachings properly encourage men and women to live as celibates. This is because they know they have to travel the path of restoration as single people up to a certain point.

The Unification Church recognizes the necessity of chastity in the religious life. Many of you get married and then separate for three years. In the secular world, lovers don't even want to be separated for one night, whether they are married or not. But you are setting a different tradition. You get married one day, and then the next you go out to work for your mission. After three years of going in different directions, you come back together. By then, you have become purified and holy, like saints. You have learned how to discipline yourselves and to withstand the temptation of love.

You want to do the will of God so much that you have gained the strength to overcome the temptation of satanic love. That is the result of Unification Church discipline. People in the Unification Church understand that the ultimate restoration is that of their love. You know that you will someday receive the genuine, pure, *agape* love of God. But you also know that you must purify yourself and get rid of your stained aspects. By the power of your determination, you go through a purification period. As godly men and women, you must be able to resist all temptation of satanic love.

This is the destiny of all people. No one can avoid it, but it is not an easy path. That is why so many religions have arisen throughout history to help man walk the reverse direction toward God.

True Love is the Purpose of Life

The title of this sermon is pointing to something very simple. Human beings are created from love and go back to love. All things take place at one beginning point and are then multiplied. Thus all women started from one woman; all men started from one man. The process of development and multiplication started at one point and will continue forever.

The purpose of our life, both coming and going, is simply love. We begin as embryos, we develop and then we experience life. In our lives we are destined to return to that point of unity in love, through which another embryo is formed. Every person is born alone, and grows up and forms a couple, but then each person dies alone.

Everyone is born from two parents; no one is his own origin. Centering upon the parents' love, the children come into existence. The cells of the embryo multiply hundreds of billions of times to form a new baby. What is the value of that child? His value comes from the fact that he is a participant in and a part of his parents' love. Our lives depend entirely upon the love of our parents; if our parents did something to exclude us from their love, we would never have existed. There is no form of life which does not naturally seek to produce its fruit, its offspring.

Since the child is a part of the love between the father and mother, he inherits all his vital elements from them. When the parents look at their children they can see everything of value within themselves because those children are the embodiments of themselves. Also the love from the past, present and future are contained within those children.

Children want to embrace and cling to their parents, not because somebody teaches them to, but because of the force of nature. That is what the universe is propelling them to do. Likewise, the law of the universe dictates that parents love and nurture their children. Even without our being aware of this law, we are guided by it. Of course, people do neglect and hurt their children because of the invasion of Satan. Fallen people are the helpless victims of Satan, and this is the source of their agony.

In spite of humanity's invasion by Satan, there is a natural tendency for people to protect and support mothers with children. Likewise, when hunters see an animal who is caring for its offspring, they will not kill it. That is because of the influence of universal law, springing from God. We can look at another example. There are men who have been convicted of terrible crimes and sentenced by society to die. Even though such a man did a terrible thing, his mother will weep for him and wish his life could be spared. Society will naturally respect and sympathize with the feelings of that mother, regardless of how terrible the crime her son committed. The man may go to the electric chair, yet his mother's heart will never change and the universe itself will protect her and seek to comfort her.

When a baby is inside the mother's womb, it receives everything it needs. It is developing every part of itself — eyes, hair, limbs — within that womb. The contribution of the father and the mother enable the baby to develop everything it needs to become a functioning human being. As the baby grows and the mother gets bigger and bigger, the husband doesn't resent his wife's size. Instead, he will do everything to show his respect and try to protect her. In fact, that is one time when a man really enjoys "ugliness" in his wife. She may be unshapely, but she is about to give birth to the seed of their love. Every part of her is swelling up, yet for all of that the husband appreciates her even more. That is because his wife's body is fulfilling its purpose. No husband of true love will ever be angry with his wife for losing her shape because of pregnancy. Nothing can surpass the sacredness and value of that woman giving birth to the fruit of their love.

God created everything within the universe for the purpose of love. He did not seek for greater material wealth, more knowledge, or more power over others. Just like us, God needs love. Thus, we can clearly understand God's agony. Although He created mankind, He has never received the fruits of His love.

As the absolute subjective Being, God needs an absolute object. Who is that supposed to be? Man and woman. Why were men and women created with both a physical and a spiritual body, instead of just one or the other? God as subject wanted to be able to communicate with the spirit of man, which was to be subjective over the physical body of man. The spiritual body of man was supposed to vibrate in resonance with the love of God, giving direction to the actions of the physical body. True love is the vibrating power with which God reaches out to man, trying to guide him into resonance with Him.

Humanity's ability to respond to the true love of God was lost because of the fall. People cannot even recognize God's true love, much less vibrate with it. The whole purpose of salvation is to restore that ability of human beings to vibrate with the love of God. Once the spiritual body of man can receive the vibration of God's love, his whole self will resound with it. His entire physical body will respond to God's stimuli. That would be the total satisfaction of love. Nothing more could be desired by anyone.

God created Adam and Eve in the same way as the other forms of life — from embryos. Only after a child grows up can he truly become one with the rest of the universe; until then, he is incomplete. As Adam and Eve reached puberty, life began to take on new meaning. Just like teenagers today, they felt the newness of romantic, poetic yearnings. They began to think about exploring the entire world and searching for adventure. They began to think about love, as well.

A man and woman truly in love will feel like engulfing each other, penetrating each other totally. God feels the same desire. Had Adam and Eve not fallen, God, Adam, and Eve together would have been intoxicated with love. God would have embraced Adam and Eve with the strongest power of true love. Nothing could have separated them at that point.

The love between the spouses meets at the central point and the children's love toward their parents joins with them. The love between people is the minus aspect. Once that minus aspect reaches the central point, the plus element of God's love will automatically come down to join with it. This is how the purpose of life was to be fulfilled.

Heaven is to be occupied by the fruit of these seeds. In spirit world these fruits automatically achieve unity and harmony with God. There will be no element which goes against God. The only purpose of being born into this world is to bear the fruits of love. As soon as a person does that, he can go to spirit world and live eternally. Life on earth is like a flicker of a second compared to the eternal life in Heaven.

We can see this purpose exemplified in the trees. They do not bear blossoms all 365 days of the year. Their time to blossom is only very short, a matter of days; then they bear their fruit. Since fruit requires all the nourishment the tree can draw from the earth and the sky, trees absorb all the nutrition they possibly can from their environment. They must absorb it with a harmonious, loving spirit; they do not have the ability to take from their environment with a spirit of selfishness and destructiveness.

Whether it is a plant, an animal, or a man — or even God — everyone exists in the direct line of love. They all center upon love in the process of bearing fruit. Positive and negative elements must come together with the attitude of love if they are to be consistent with the direction of God's love. Thus the spirit world is the world of love because it is the continuation of this world. The spirit world is filled with the air of love. As long as you have perfected your seed and fruit, you are welcomed and free anywhere you go in spirit world. No element there will reject you. But unless your seed is perfected, you are a foreign element there.

If Adam and Eve had not fallen, humankind would never have experienced such agony. The children would only have had to follow the parents in their love, and when the time came, the children as perfected fruit would automatically live in eternal happiness in spirit world. This was the original path for which humanity was created. Thus, no religion was supposed to be necessary; the difficult ways we endure now would never have been necessary either.

To Overcome the Secular Standard of Love, Love Your Enemies

Certainly we see love in the satanic world; in fact, it permeates that world. But we see a different kind of love in the Heavenly world. The love which is outside of God's realm knows only how to retaliate against one's enemies. Those who love each other fight against their common enemies. But in God's world, we love even the enemy and we never retaliate against others. When we love even our enemy, Satan must run away because he has no foundation to claim anything as his own.

Humanity has this problem of love to solve before it can reach the ideal. This is what Jesus tried to teach. He was telling people that if they wanted to go east, they should go west. If they wanted to live, they had to die. If they wanted to die, they would live. This paradox can be understood once we understand the difference between the original state and the way it became inverted. Although everyone may think they are moving toward the west, it is actually the east they are pursuing and vice versa. So we know enough now to go the right direction.

As Christians, we should love everybody. First we should love our enemies, whether some personal enemy or some enemy on the family level. We should love them more than anybody else. The same is true for the country —a country should love its enemy country more than any other country. Otherwise we cannot go to Heaven because Heaven will reject us.

According to this reasoning, what is the biggest enemy, greater than any other? It is the enemy who put the entire universe into chaos and destruction, the biggest enemy of all — Satan. We should love even that enemy. We should love him because God has been loving him; that is exactly God's position. Satan robbed God of His love and His family; he destroyed the possibility of God's country and God's universe. Satan is truly God's arch-enemy. Since God is omnipotent, He could ruthlessly destroy Satan if He wanted to. However, God did not and would not do that because His love never operates out of hatred and destruction.

By our own power alone, we cannot possibly break out of Satan's bondage. Satan is holding man so tightly; we could say that, on a scale of 1 to 10, Satan's power is a 9. The source of Satan's power is satanic love which is illicit but still very powerful over human beings. The only power greater than satanic love is that of God's love. That love is 100% powerful; it is a 10 on the scale. This 100% love cannot be found any other place except with God. Salvation can only come from the original, 100% love.

Original love is the only hope for humanity because no other power can break our bondage to Satan. Even though he is the fallen archangel, Satan cannot oppose the original love. When you approach Satan with original love, he has two options: either to surrender to you, or to go away and never bother you again. This is the covenant between God and Satan, based upon the original principles of the universe. It is the law which binds Satan as well as God himself. Therefore the religions of history have had the basic purpose of pursuing that original love.

Directly or indirectly, all men and women have sought to regain the original love; that has been the dream of humanity. Idealistic people have always dreamed of societies, nations, and a world centered upon original love.

God knew that the power of religion would be the force to eliminate Satan at the last days. However, religion always has the tendency to become diluted by secular powers. For that reason, God promised that He would send the Messiah. The Messiah comes to bring the fulfillment of God's ancient covenant and law — he brings original love. Centered upon that original love, he will organize original families, societies, and nations; he will establish a new earthly order. This is the very purpose of the Messiah.

The foundation for the Messiah has to be Christianity because Christianity is the only religion to understand that the true nature of God is that of Father. Jesus was the only holy man who called himself the only-begotten son of God. That means Jesus alone knew God's original love. Jesus was indeed the Messiah because God was his Father and he was His only-begotten son. Thus the religion that he founded must become the foundation for the second coming of the Messiah, when God's original love will be fulfilled.

Christianity had to become the most widespread religion in the world because God has a big stake in it; He has a plan for fulfilling His dispensation through it. Unfortunately, traditional Christianity is divided and confused, and there are many mistaken ideas, such as that Jesus came only to die. Likewise, many Christians are content to worry only about their individual salvation, disregarding the matters of this world for one's own little cubbyhole ''upstairs.'' The concept of being saved by faith alone is not right either; one must fulfill love in order to go to Heaven. Without the power of love, one can never be separated from satanic bondage.

Vertical Love of Parents, Children, and Grandparents

Life comes to this earth, starting from love. As it develops, it makes many connections, like a tree developing branches and leaves. While a person is growing, he is learning to love. A husband learns to love his wife, and a wife her husband; together they learn to love their children; and the children learn to love their parents. By experiencing all these facets of life, each grows and eventually returns to where he began—to love. This is the purpose of our life here on earth; it is where we have come from and where we are going.

We must realize the principle that is governing this universe. Even animals will protect their children at the sacrifice of their own lives. Certainly that feeling is much stronger in man. If any loving parent has a choice between dying himself or letting his child die, certainly he would prefer to die himself. The vertical relationship is so important that it enables man to sacrifice his horizontal existence. The relationship between husband and wife is horizontal but the parent and child have a vertical relationship. A person will prefer to give up his horizontal relationships for the sake of the child. Likewise, the horizontal axis must adjust itself to the vertical one.

Therefore, we have the commandment to love God more than anyone, including our spouse. That is because God is the source of the vertical line and the conjugal relationship is a horizontal one. After loving God that much and then loving your spouse, your horizontal line will automatically create a 90 degree angle and find its balance. Each of the parents should love their children more than they love each other. This is for the same reason. They should love each other only on the foundation of loving their children more.

Whatever God loves the most, you also will love the most. Since God loves the children more than the couple and because He loves the "whole purpose" more, then we also love them more. First we love our parents; then we love our children; finally, we love our husband or wife — in that order. This order will be reflected through the levels of family, clan, nation, and so on to the cosmos.

Many modern Americans have the attitude that children are a burden to the pleasure of the husband and wife. They think that their own enjoyment is the purpose of their life. But if that way of thinking becomes dominant within a culture, the society will quickly decline. We must return to God's principles. God's way is actually the way that works the best in a practical sense, as well. The most general way of stating God's principles is "Live for the sake of others, not oneself."

Your grandparents have the tendency to love you even more than they love their own offspring. This is because the grandparents are one step closer to God than the parents. In God's culture, the grandparents would be like the king and queen to the family. The children would greet the grandparents first in the morning. With such a pattern, God and the universe can preserve that family. No matter what, we can never forsake our parents or our children. Although it's possible to get a divorce from your spouse you can never be divorced from your vertical lineage; thus you must respect and preserve it. This is the law of the universe.

How far away this proud American culture is from God's way of life! You too, wanted to have parents who would sacrifice everything for your sake, but most of you did not have such parents. Too many husbands and wives only think about embracing each other, creating their own heaven. But in that "heaven," their parents and their children are crying for their love. Certainly that is hell, not heaven. We clearly know what must occur. It is nothing less than a revolution. You must quickly change the prevailing attitudes to the original one.

Every form of love is found within the family. Within that realm, God dwells. If this is realized perfectly, those family members do not need to search for anything more. They are qualified to live forever in the heavenly Kingdom.

Such a family will extend their love toward all things. They will love animals, the plant world, and all of the creation. Before God ever created human beings, He created the world of creation. That was because humans were supposed to gain the sensation and knowledge of God's love from the animals and plants. Everything is directed ultimately for love—the birds and all of creation are there to remind us of love. The natural world is a textbook of love.

Connect yourselves with your parents and your grandparents to such a degree that your grandparents will grab hold of you and say, "I cannot live without you." Likewise, your parents will say, "I can give up everything but not you." When you become the fruit of true love within such a family, you can go anywhere and be completely welcome. You can even jump up on the head of God and He will love you all the more. But in order to make your parents and grandparents love you in such a fashion, you must first love your parents, your grandparents, and your children with the same intensity. Your spouse must be willing to love and serve your parents.

There is no room in the Unification Church for senior citizens homes.

You must clearly understand what to expect from your grandparents. A baby wets his diaper and makes a lot of mess, and similarly, when people are old and about to go to spirit world, they may behave like babies once again. They may even wet their diapers again. We are expected to take care of them just as we take care of our own babies. There is no difference except that the grandparents are even more precious. Those who care for their parents and grandparents in such a way will find themselves well prepared for the spirit world.

The whole purpose of life here on earth is to learn how to love. You should love your parents, your children, and your spouse with the intensity of pure, first love. That will bring total fulfillment to you and to your environment. How beautiful it is to embrace your elderly grandparents! In spite of the great age difference, you can love each other as if you belonged to the same generation. The value of such love goes beyond any amount of money or any other thing. When God sees such a loving scene, he will bow down his own head in thanks.

It is such a beautiful sight to God when 90-year-old grandparents are embracing their great-grandchildren, who are just babies. But in modern society in America, many parents discourage the grandparents from taking an active part in the lives of the children. They complain about the children being "spoiled" and so forth, but that is going against the law of nature. Children need the love of grandparents and vice-versa.

Each person needs his passport of love enabling him to enjoy total freedom when he goes to spirit world. Where can we get this passport? Only through our own children's, parents', and grandparents' approval. They have to tell us we are worthy of Heaven. Can you name any other kind of love which I didn't mention today? All the types of love are included within the family — including the love of country and the universe.

Understand that you are creating the foundation for the fulfillment of your life's purpose, which is to connect your love to everyone in the world. That means you must love your enemies. If you are white, then you must love black and yellow people. If you are German, you must love Americans and vice versa.

If any of you couples have had the habit of fighting among yourselves, you should stop that. There is no other happiness except within your own family; the Kingdom of Heaven must be realized there. If the whole world were dwelling in peace but you and your spouse were in conflict, you would have nothing to do with the world's peace. Everything happens within your own family, the unit of the Kingdom of Heaven.

God bless you!

4

GOD'S WILL
AND CHRISTMAS

Today is Christmas, and people around the world are celebrating the birth of Jesus Christ. When we think of Jesus, we know that he was not born with an individual purpose, like the average person, but rather that he came to this earth to save the world. Because of the fall, humankind clearly needs a Savior in order to return to God. Humankind is alienated from God, and everyone must go through Jesus in order to return to Him.

It is most important in celebrating this day of Christmas to know the purpose of the coming of Jesus Christ 2,000 years ago. Without knowing that purpose clearly this celebration is meaningless, so this morning I would like to deliver a message on the topic, "God's Will and Christmas."

When we ask if God's original intention for this world has been completely fulfilled, the obvious answer is no. The will of God was originally thwarted because of the human fall. Through history fallen humankind has been searching for the ultimate fulfillment of the will of God and the purpose of creation. As this providence has been advancing on many different levels of the individual, family, society, nation and world, God's original will or blueprint has never changed.

God is eternal, unchanging, absolute and unique; therefore, the will of God is also eternal, unchanging, absolute and unique. God cannot compromise His original standard because of human failure. He cannot come down to the level of sinful humanity; humans must be lifted up to the level of God.

Jesus Came to Realize the Kingdom
of God on Earth

Since the fall, God's will has focused on the goal of restoration. God is determined to save mankind, to show people how to get out of the fallen state and into the original ideal of creation. That is restoration or the providence of salvation. Throughout history people have not been in a position to save themselves; salvation comes instead from God. God must send a Savior to reveal God's original ideal of creation to the world. That man was Jesus Christ.

As you know, God's original intention for this world would not only have been the perfection of an individual, but would have brought the perfection of the family. That would have expanded into the perfection of the clan, society, nation and the world. Had Adam and Eve reached perfection without falling, today's world would be entirely different. We would not see all the disgusting sights that we witness every day. Neither would we see the language barriers and the national barriers separating people. Furthermore, every individual would live to realistically attain perfection and could clearly map out his or her own way of life to reach the ultimate Kingdom of Heaven. The problem today is that humans do not know the living God and lack proper direction. People live random, wandering lives. In the original ideal this would never be; everyone would be guided into perfection in a way perfectly parallel with the will of God, and no one could or would wish to live outside that will.

If there had been no fall, humankind would be citizens of the Kingdom of God on earth. The citizens of the Kingdom of God will start their lives here on earth, and after they consummate their lives here they will automatically be elevated into the Kingdom of God in Heaven, where they will continue as families.

There was always a blueprint in the mind of God, the original plan that always has been and will always remain perfect, even though the physical realization of these plans has never yet been seen. Jesus prayed, "Thy Kingdom come, Thy will be done on earth as it is in heaven." Jesus knew the perfection of God's will in Heaven and he brought that will to earth, coming to establish perfection here. That was God's plan.

The Living Jesus Was the Perfect Mediator of Salvation

Jesus Christ came for the will of God, to transmit God's will to the chosen nation of Israel. God was moving in a certain direction and Jesus Christ was moving parallel to that direction, so certainly the people of Israel were supposed to move in a way parallel to Jesus. If all three had been moving parallel in one direction, God's ultimate will could have been fulfilled in that nation. God and Jesus were united, and all that was needed was to have the people of Israel unite with Jesus. After fulfillment on the national level, expansion of that fulfillment to the worldwide level would have been assured.

Jesus came as priest to be received by the people of Israel. He brought the great opportunity to fulfill the condition for restoration of the garden of Eden. Everything was lost in the garden of Eden, but everything could have been restored by the chosen nation of Israel if they had united with the Messiah. The bloody battles that occurred for many centuries after Jesus' appearance should never have been. God had prepared Israel for many thousands of years to be ready to accept the Messiah when he appeared. Although Jesus did not appear in the way that most of the Jews of his time expected, they still should have had the wisdom to accept and work together with the Messiah the day he came. Thus, John the Baptist in preparing the way for Jesus, declared to the world, "Repent, for the Kingdom of God is at hand." Jesus repeated the same warning, with his first words being, "Repent, for the Kingdom of God is at hand."

The Messiah was able to understand and reason with the heart of God so that he could be united with God's love. The exceptional human qualities of his personality allowed him to connect with the people of Israel. He was the bridge between God and all the fallen world, and by accepting him the people would have been accepting and uniting with God. God's will was the acceptance of the Messiah, not his rejection. Jesus was truly the Messiah, and through the total obedience of the people he should have been given the power to lead Israel.

Jesus' death was not suicide; it was an execution. Today the Christian doctrine preaches salvation by the blood of Jesus. But it must be asked whether God and Jesus subscribe to this doctrine. In the Bible is recorded the story of a prostitute who was condemned to death and about to be stoned. Jesus said to the people gathered around her, "Whoever is without sin, let him cast the first stone." Everyone self-consciously dropped their stones. After everyone had drifted away in shame, Jesus spoke to the accused woman, saying, "Has no one condemned you? Neither do I condemn you. Go and sin no more." What does this mean? By his own words Jesus offered forgiveness. Even before Jesus shed one drop of blood there was already salvation. No one had to wait for Jesus to die. There was salvation in accepting the word of Jesus. That's in the Bible. He did not give a raincheck by saying, "I will forgive you and save you, but wait until I die on the cross." Jesus offered salvation to everyone by the word of God. God's plan of salvation does not require bloodshed. The word salvation means that the garden of Eden shall be here on earth, with living men, women, and families. What we need is living consummation, not bloodshed and death.

Adam, Jesus, and the Second Coming Are for the Same Purpose

God has not yet seen the perfection of His original plan here on earth, however, even after the coming of Jesus Christ. Because of the crucifixion Jesus could not accomplish the full purpose of his coming, the realization of the ideal of Eden. It was not at all God's original plan to fulfill the ideal by killing the Messiah. If that was indeed God's method, then just sending him to a nation that was unprepared to understand him would have been sufficient. Sacrifice is sometimes necessary, but God did not intend the sacrifice of human life as the key to complete salvation. Because of the crucifixion Jesus Christ was not able to bring humankind to the fullest degree of individual perfection or to family, societal or national perfection. Therefore, it is most logical that the Messiah must come a second time.

What will Jesus do when he comes? Will he come to wipe out the world? The word "judgment" is frequently misunderstood to mean that God will wipe out everything in anger. That is not the purpose of the Messiah's coming a second time. The whole purpose is to fulfill the mission that was left undone 2,000 years ago, to work for individual, family, societal, national and world perfection. Judgment is the constructive work of God to see the fulfillment of the Kingdom of God here on earth.

The work of God is realistic and physical. By interpreting the Bible literally, many Christians anticipate Jesus' appearance in the sky, but there are problems with this view. People perceive God as being supernatural, someone who could perform even the miracle of bringing Jesus on the clouds. But why would Christianity be necessary in that case? Why would faith be necessary? Why didn't God use supernatural power to build up the Kingdom of God in the first place? Why has He had to wait for 6,000 years to accomplish this?

I want you to know that God's will in sending Jesus Christ 2,000 years ago perfectly parallels the coming of Adam in the garden of Eden. The Lord of the Second Advent will come for the same purpose. In other words, God's will, Adam's purpose, Jesus' purpose and the purpose of the Second Coming are all the same. Truth is unchanging, being the beginning and the end. The will of God cannot be changed or tarnished by time but will be the same forever. God has a formula, and when it is fulfilled God will seal it. That particular formula is still there, unfulfilled; God is waiting for man to fulfill that pure, unadulterated standard.

Jesus the True Man, One with God

What is a true man? Is the President of the United States automatically a true man? The true man is one who perfectly fits God's framework, meaning that if God is round, that true man is perfectly round, and if God is square, that true man is perfectly square. From day to night, from eternity, to eternity he will not deviate from that standard.

How do we know Jesus was a true man? He didn't write a big sign on his forehead or get a Ph.D. He didn't have any extraordinary size or power. Why do we know him to be a true man? We know Jesus was a true man because his way of life was parallel with the will of God and fit perfectly the description of God's way of life. We know that Jesus Christ was born solely for the will of God, that he lived solely for the will of God, and that he died solely for the will of God. At the critical moment of Jesus' death on the cross he died as a Messiah and with the dignity of a Messiah, not as an ordinary man, a sad man, or a man taking cover. Jesus could not give up the will of God by resenting the people's adamant opposition to his efforts to save them. He deeply felt, "Even though the Roman Empire opposes me now, it shall receive my mercy. Even though the Israelites oppose me, they shall receive my mercy." Therefore, Jesus had room to forgive them, room to pray for them and to embrace them.

Jesus was a true man because he perfectly lived the life of God. He was a walking God. There was no separation between God and Jesus, and because no one can destroy God no one can destroy Jesus Christ. The crucifixion was not his destruction; God manifested the power of resurrection so that the world could see that Jesus was never destroyed.

What Attitude Is Needed in Order
to Receive the Messiah?

Since the fulfillment of perfection was not obtained in Israel, God prepared Christianity as the second Israel, as the foundation upon which the second Messiah could come. To lay that foundation is the task of Christianity. The ultimate goal of Christians the world over is to receive the Messiah. Many Christians think that the Messiah will command extraordinary miracles to happen which will solve all the world's problems in one moment, instantly making the world the Kingdom of God. This is their ambiguous understanding, but it could not possibly be so.

When the Messiah comes the second time, he will start from the very bottom of man's situation and advance step by step to the height of the Kingdom. He brings the pattern which the rest of the world should follow and he will not compromise with the world. He will initiate the final showdown between good and evil. According to God's original standard, are modern-day Christians ready to be lifted up to the Kingdom of God in heaven as perfected men and women? Not at all. They must transform themselves and change to fit into the pattern that the Messiah will bring; as the second Israel, Christians are to be the first people to change themselves into that model.

Many Christians have been steadfastly waiting for Christ to come again—on a cloud. If he came on a cloud, perhaps wearing a parachute, he would be recognized and honored as the Messiah, undoubtedly. But isn't there any chance at all that he would not come on a cloud, but would appear as a regular person? After all what kind of a Messiah would mankind need: one who descends from the clouds as a supernatural virtually non-human being; or one who is one of us, with the same flesh and the same mind? Certainly, people need a real person to relate with in the position of Christ.

Jesus described himself as "the way, the truth, and the life." It really didn't make any difference which manner he came into the world — even if he had come on the clouds, clouds are not the way, the truth and the life. It was Jesus himself who was important, nothing else. However he came to the world, he taught clearly about the way to live, the truth for mankind and how to gain life. Also, Jesus was "the love'; he did not say that, but he was the love for the world.

Would humanity prefer to receive a Messiah who came dramatically on a cloud, without teaching and being all those things which Jesus was, or a Messiah who came normally but was able to convey those precious understandings? Certainly, humanity would value the second kind of Messiah.

How well do you know the will of God? Many Christians are convinced that God's will for them is to seek only their own chunk of Heaven, and they could care less about the fate of the rest of the world. Meanwhile the nation and the world are crumbling, and instead of feeling responsible, they expect God to handle everything. That is not true Christianity.

I want you to know clearly that God's and Jesus' target is the world, not just one man, one race, one people or one nation. God intended the Messiah to accomplish the fulfillment of perfection, not to create a multitude of denominations. He still is determined to achieve that one ultimate goal of perfection and unity between people.

How can a divided and bickering Christianity exemplify Jesus' ideal?

I have seen what the Kindgom of God is like in the spirit world, and ultimately you too will see that God's Kingdom is not organized in the same divided way that religions are here. Such separation is truly contrary to the will of God. The conflict and division between religious people has been carried over into spirit world and brings grief to God. Yet that has been conventional faith.

How Can You Become True Sons and Daughters of Christ?

We believe in Jesus Christ as the Savior and Messiah because we also want to become the sons or daughters who can fulfill the will of God. Jesus died for the sake of the mission, not just to acquire his own chunk of Heaven. Therefore, don't ever worry about your own heaven, but worry about bringing down the Kingdom of God to your society and to this world. If you are like that, when you say to God, ''I don't want to go to the Kingdom of God,'' God will chase after you and personally install you in the highest position in His Kingdom.

Jesus never complained to God about the rebelliousness of the very people he had been sent to save and never ceased caring about them. That was not Jesus' heart. Jesus knew clearly that his mission was not just the salvation of Israel but of the world. Jesus as the son of God was perfectly united with God in will and in heart. Because of that oneness, Jesus Christ could willingly die for the rest of the world.

How can you become the true sons and daughters of Christ? By becoming perfectly one with Jesus Christ, one with his spirit and one with his heart. If you are perfectly united with Jesus Christ, you can be a willing sacrifice for the salvation of the rest of the world. God would be most pleased to hear Jesus pray, "God, Your goal is world salvation. Please use me and my Christian brothers and sisters as Your sacrifice to fulfill Your work." The true Christians are those who are willing to sacrifice themselves, their own church and their denomination for the fulfillment of the will of God for world salvation.

Looking at the 2,000 years of Christian history, we can see that millions of Christians have prayed deeply and unselfishly to God. In the beginning of Christianity, what do you think was the predominant prayer? Their constant plea to God was, "Oh, Lord, please send Your son again as You promised." That was very different from the kinds of prayers most people are praying today: "Lord, please help my family to be prosperous; bless my church," etc.

A true Christian could not pray for God's help and blessing for only his family. Those who pray only for their own chunk of God's blessing will not end up in Heaven. After knowing the truth of God's situation we can only pray, "God, I am ready to be Your sacrifice. Use me as Your instrument; fulfill Your will for world salvation through me." Such people will create the Kingdom of God.

The Reality of the First Christmas

To better know the heart of Jesus, let us recall his situation at the first Christmas. Today there are so many churches which are observing the birth of Christ with celebrations and rejoicing. The traditional attitude has been one of praise for the way in which the Messiah was born in a stable and laid in a manger on straw. But how could humankind be proud of the son of God being born in a stable?

The Jews were prepared by God to receive and assist Jesus, but did people really have the slightest idea of who Jesus was and what they were supposed to do in order to help him fulfill the will of God? They did not know a thing. Was there anyone who understood Jesus' mission as an individual, his mission to restore his family, the nation around his family, and finally the whole world? It is very clear that there was no one, either secular or religious, who helped Jesus accomplish his mission.

If there was anyone at all who understood Jesus and helped him it was God Himself. God knew, but no one else except Jesus understood his responsibility. Was God content and happy while looking down on His son born in a stable, crying out in the cold, with no one around him knowing what they were supposed to do, and with Satan searching intently to find some way to stop him? Could God feel easy in that situation?

Let us go back and think in a little more detail about what the immediate environment was like. Mary was Jesus' mother, but Joseph was not his father. When Joseph married her, Mary was pregnant and Joseph knew that it was not his child she carried. Joseph did not know anything except what he was told in one short dream. He was a righteous man so he married Mary as he was instructed to do by an angel, but how long do you think Joseph could feel righteous and happy about it? Don't you think he kept on wondering and repeatedly asking her, "Whose baby is it?" Could Mary just casually answer, "Oh, it was conceived by the Holy Spirit, so you should be happy'? Even if Mary had truthfully said that, do you think that Joseph would have responded with joy?

Be realistic and imagine yourself in that position. Suppose everyone respects you as a very generous man, but you have to marry some woman who is pregnant with someone else's child. If she told you that it was conceived by the Holy Spirit then perhaps one day you would not have resentment, but could you still feel generous for all the years afterward? If one of you were in Joseph's situation, hearing gossip and criticism all around, would you feel very happy and content with Mary? Would you be glad to serve the child once he was born and sacrifice to protect him from evil?

It is likely that Joseph asked Mary many times whose baby she carried, because he was curious and because he tried to understand. But remember that at that time an unmarried woman who became pregnant was required by Mosaic law to be stoned for committing adultery. At first Joseph probably thought he would understand, but in the long run he could not accept the situation. Do you think that their relationship was happy for very long? It is probable that they quarreled and distrusted each other rather than fully understanding and cooperating in love.

Once Jesus was born the rift no doubt became even greater, and Joseph looked upon Jesus as something which was not wanted and which had ruined his relationship with Mary. Judging from the reality of human nature this was the situation that probably existed all through Jesus' life. Because of their parents' attitude towards Jesus, even his own brothers and sisters would not have respected him, much less have thought that he was the son of God. They would have even treated him worse than other children because he was different.

The Bible records that Mary and Joseph took Jesus to the temple in Jerusalem for Passover, and when they left the city, they didn't even bother to check whether Jesus was with them. They became aware of his absence only after a full day's journey. Even in an average family, can you imagine parents leaving a boy of Jesus' age all alone in a crowded city?

We can safely assume that Mary and Joseph quarreled over this. Joseph might have said, ''Forget about it. Let's leave,'' and Mary had to go along. But because Mary was insistent, and Joseph knew that she would not yield, they turned back again to find Jesus and bring him home with them.

While Mary was pregnant and while the disharmony between Mary and Joseph continued, don't you think that rumors went around the whole neighborhood about how they often fought? In a neighborhood as close together as an ancient Jewish village, chances are that everybody knew that Mary and Joseph did not get along for some reason. The high priest Zechariah and all the relatives at least knew and disapproved of the situation.

Joseph's family knew that Jesus was not really one of them, and even though they might not have discussed it in front of him, Jesus was not respected. Even now in a society as permissive as America's, if a girl has a baby whose father is not known then there is some talk about it. A much harsher situation prevailed in Jesus' time, when an unwed mother was punishable by death. Certainly there would have been cruel gossip. Could Jesus have grown up happy and contented like an average child under these circumstances, or can you imagine that Jesus was caught in an unbearable situation? Every child that Jesus played with certainly must have made comments about things heard from his parents. Jesus just could not have had normal relationships with other children.

Nevertheless, the fact remains that Jesus was born to save all of the people. He was the only begotten son of God, and his object of salvation was exactly the people who ostracized him. The way the King of kings was mistreated and misunderstood by the people around him was vastly different from God's ideal for Jesus.

What Kind of Person Could Have Consoled Jesus?

Did anyone around Jesus try to defend him? There is not one account which records such dedication. Jesus was mistreated and persecuted by his own family because they completely lacked any understanding of who he was. Even without his being King of kings and the son of God, was he even treated as well as an ordinary child?

Common sense would say that even on holidays or special occasions no one made special clothing or gifts and presented them to Jesus. The brothers and sisters who were more favored by Joseph might have gotten something, but even Mary was reluctant to anger Joseph by giving anything to Jesus. Of course, Jesus must have wanted to wear the special clothes and eat the special food of that time, as we all do, but no one would give him any.

Jesus definitely knew that he was special. He heard what the people around him thought about him, but his own self-image was completely different. From the time he was small he could never talk openly in his own way. The only consolation he could seek was in communication with God, and he spent most of his time praying to God and seeking His guidance. As a result, Jesus became stronger and stronger in this period, and circumstances compelled him in only one direction — toward God and the realization of His ideal. He knew that mankind's thinking was vastly different from God's and that it had to be corrected; he also knew that society understood nothing about what God wanted and that he himself would have to change it. Because of his adverse circumstances Jesus prayed intensely to God, to the point where God could talk to him and teach him what he would need for his future work.

Under these circumstances, do you think that during Jesus' years on earth anyone celebrated his birthday with real joy? As Jesus grew older and knew more and more clearly who God was and what his own mission was supposed to be, his heart became heavier and more agonized and his environment became more difficult to tolerate.

The most precious friend for Jesus would have been the person who came to him, not with many presents or words of congratulations, but rather with a tearful heart to console him in his situation and to discuss with him what he was going to do in the future. If someone like this had been there then Jesus would have been far happier than if someone had come with presents. That person could have been one of his own brothers or sisters. Knowing his hidden suffering, he or she could have brought just a small piece of cake wrapped in a handkerchief to give to Jesus on his birthday, saying, "The people don't understand you, but I will try to help you. You must not be disappointed." Jesus certainly would have welcomed such a person far more than someone who came with a fancy present for him and then went away. If there had been one such brother or sister in Jesus' family, then Jesus would have remembered him for a long time and would have spoken about it.

When Jesus felt despondent, he had to pray to God more intensely, and being moved by Jesus' fervent prayer, God taught him, "You will later become great in this way and rise to this particular position." That's the way it was supposed to be anyway, with God telling him many things in detail. Because of these experiences, Jesus knew that God was his best friend and the one closest to him, quite unlike Joseph or Mary, or even his brothers and sisters.

Jesus was very serious in thinking about the national situation at that time, praying about how to change things. He knew what God had in His plan for himself, the Israelites and all humankind. God is spirit, but by having a body Jesus could understand the existing situation of the world, and he knew that he had to be the central point to bring that world back to God. Do you think that he wanted very much for someone to show some understanding, or that he wanted to hear even one word of love spoken to him, knowing that without him no one had any chance to return to God? Jesus yearned to hear the high priest say, "We must prepare ourselves to receive you, because that's the only way for us to return to God."

Do we know of anyone who understood and said this? To the last, the people did not understand him, and as a result Jesus was crucified. When Jesus died on the cross he was unspeakably despondent. Jesus was made absolutely desperate by the people's lack of understanding, but how would God have felt at losing him from the earth, and at having to prepare once more for thousands of years to send the Messiah?

When Jesus was in the deepest anguish on the cross God's feeling matched his exactly. There could not be any difference whatever. When you are really indignant and absolutely furious inside, can you even think about giving happiness or blessing? When someone comes near you at such a time do you feel like being generous and open-hearted? This is exactly the feeling God had as He watched His son dying on the cross.

With this understanding, we know how much deep pain God is caused by the traditional belief of Christian churches that Jesus came to die, As I said, it is our relationship to the living Jesus that brings fellowship with God. Hence our salvation comes through the resurrection and our relationship with the resurrected Jesus, not through the blood of the cross. Yet even the resurrection could by no means compensate for the damage done by Christ's lonely crucifixion. God's ultimate will required God's chosen people to unite with Jesus in the flesh and go with him to fulfill the Kingdom of God on earth. His death blocked the providence for world restoration and made a Second Coming necessary.

In this desperate situation Jesus realized the significance of what had happened and said, "I will come back again." Can you now understand that it is not possible for Jesus to come again on the clouds in a happy way and magically restore the world? When millions of people sing hymns and exchange presents and wish each other good fortune on his birthday, is Jesus overjoyed and happy? While he loves his people, there remains deep in his heart the painful memories of the failure of that part of his mission, which he only could have fulfilled if people had welcomed and consoled him while on earth.

The True Celebration of Christmas

Is there anyone who can celebrate Jesus' birthday in its true meaning, understanding his situation and what he was supposed to do? There are millions of people who celebrate Christmas because everyone else does; but who knows Jesus' situation and then commemorates the day? The only celebration which would have meaning for him would be when one who suffers more than Jesus and is more despondent than Jesus himself comes to Jesus, were to say, ''I have a difficult situation but your situation is much worse. I would like to celebrate your birthday nevertheless. Forget about your sorrow for a moment.'' When Jesus sees Christians like that, he will burst into tears and momentarily celebrate his birthday.

There are many people here in this auditorium, but what kind of people are you and what are you supposed to do? Shall we get many good things by using Jesus' name, or shall we help Jesus? What is this church designed by God to do? What is the purpose of sacrificing ourselves? By sacrificing we are to fulfill the idea which Jesus pursued and thus bring everyone into unity.

At Jesus' time the people did not understand him, but today everyone can understand this realm of heart. If someone in the most lowly servant position had come to console Jesus and talk with him, Jesus would have felt much closer to him than to all the other powerful people at that time. Because that person's heart would have been closer to Jesus', he would have been close in every other way as well. Jesus wouldn't have stopped that person from coming just because he wasn't in the same noble position as Jesus; he would have embraced him right there and burst into tears. That is the realm of the heart, the standard of value which surpasses any national or societal boundary and which can link people forever.

Can people feel complete oneness simply by sitting around a plush banquet table eating steaks and good food? It is rather in the really desperate situation where everybody sheds tears together that heartfelt unity with Christ is realized. Why would you prefer the second setting? You feel drawn that way, not because you like struggle, but because Jesus feels that way and God feels that way. The only reason why everyone must also do such a thing is in order to share in whatever God has for you.

This is also true for me. People would prefer many other things, but even though the family may drift away or the society may not give a ready welcome or the world may not understand, we cannot abandon the way which God has opened for those who would follow Jesus, no matter how difficult it is. This is why I am doing what I am doing. The sole purpose for my being here is to have you follow exactly the same path as God Himself. Do you agree with that? Sometimes it is very difficult but this is the only sure way to become a friend of Jesus and of God Himself.

We chose the same way as Jesus did and in that way we can understand and participate in the friendship of God. If a woman is going to follow Jesus she can follow with the heart of Mary and relieve that situation of 2,000 years ago by trying to be the best possible Mary. If it is a man, then he should try to serve Christ in the position of Joseph. To follow Christ, a person may also follow like Jesus' own brothers and sisters, who were meant to understand him completely and love him and do the most difficult things for him. By doing this and becoming one with Jesus, Jesus and God Himself will never be able to say in the future, "I don't know you." Those who are following Christ as a real friend can console him, going over the path of thorns in this world and feeling fury at all the injustice done to him. Such people can say, "They don't understand. I will compensate for their mistakes, so don't blame them or be agonized at the situation. Try to forget about them and let's do it together." If the Messiah had had such followers then certainly God would have been able to come and unfold the rest of the dispensation. If someone came to Jesus to express regret at his difficulties then Jesus would answer, "Well, it is difficult but I can bear it. But how about you? Your path is more difficult.'' Such a flow of heart is the foundation for Heaven on earth.

The world is celebrating Christmas in its best way, but let us celebrate Christmas in the truest sense, understanding the true situation of Jesus and the meaning of his second coming, devoting all our heart and love to becoming one in love with God. Then we are the participants in all that belongs to God.

We should remind ourselves that Jesus never had one real birthday celebration when he was on earth, and it will be immensely meaningful to him to see the many people who are gathered here to celebrate in the true sense. Wouldn't you be grateful to participate in the true Christmas celebration? Do you think Jesus would be happy to see that the people gathered here have had tears and sweat staining their faces, and have gone without beautiful clothes to do God's work? Do you feel confident that Jesus would be deeply moved to see you gathered here to sing Christmas songs and wish him happy birthday?

You must know for sure that you are on the road to becoming sons and daughters of God, to whom even God and Jesus can be thankful for what you have done. Such people are the most beautiful women in the world and the greatest men. Those of you who are determined that for the rest of your lives you will stay close to the path of Christ, embracing the past and present and future until God's will is fulfilled, raise your hands. God bless you. Let us pray.

5

STONY PATH OF TEARS

What is this stony path? It is the road of providence or dispensation. No one in history or in the world today readily volunteers to walk the stony path. No individual, family, society or nation likes to walk a stony path, for they want to have a smooth road instead. People would rather drive on a highway in a scenic area instead of a desert. In the Oriental concept, man's life is compared to a journey, and people think of life in terms of a happy and peaceful, or unhappy journey. Why are some people destined to walk a stony path? The reason is quite mysterious.

This desire for a carefree life is not limited to man, but includes nature. Grass wants to grow in fertile ground with lots of sunlight and nice rain, and birds look for a comfortable dwelling where they can be at peace. All of nature wants to live in peaceful circumstances. God also would like to have a peaceful existence. It is man who sets himself apart from nature in his suffering and struggles.

There have been many great and righteous people in the past. What kind of life pattern did they have? Usually, they lived in tears, toil and hardship. Did they volunteer for that life or was it forced upon them by circumstances? Though they did not volunteer, their environment brought a hard life upon them. They lived a life of difficulty in order to overcome humanity's unhappiness. Those who pioneered the righteous path in history did so in tears and sweat.

Where does true happiness begin? Where does true peace or the ideal begin? Do true peace and righteousness begin after a life of toil and tears, or before these things? Why are they only found beyond that hill? Something went wrong. That something was the fall. Religion came into being in recognition that human life is not as it should be. Without the recognition that there was some deviation from the original world, religion could not exist. The fall reduced humankind to an abnormal and unhappy state. Religion tries to overcome that unhappy state and bring man back to normality. Therefore, religion is on a collision path with man's unhappy state, trying to shatter it into pieces.

God Labors in Grief

Is religion based on the charismatic personality of its leaders, or on God? Religion must be based on God. Is God, Who has to drive humanity onto this path of collision with unhappiness, a happy God? A human has only a limited life span, and in that brief time he has to go through much hardship and toil to overcome his unhappy state, but God has had to continue that struggle for thousands of years. Can you imagine His grief and misery in having to do so?

The fall of humankind is directly connected to the sorrow of God. Today we see people who live from day to day for fun and entertainment, but if they truly want happiness and righteousness they cannot continue that way; they must collide with their surroundings and rise above them. The first step in a life of religion is recognizing the tragedy of the fall, and trying to remedy that state. The fall brought misery not only to humanity, but to God. He has been living continually in struggle and unhappiness, but no man has recognized this.

Does the solution begin with humanity or with God? If it is only a human problem then we don't have to worry about God, and if it is only God's problem then we don't have to worry about humanity. But the problem is equally serious for both humans and God, and thus the solution must be structured in such a way as to include them both. Because the fall brought tragedy to both humanity and God, they must think along the same lines if they are to bring a solution. If God is crying then people cannot be laughing; if God is struggling over the hills then humanity cannot be skipping over flat ground.

If you are sorrowful and someone comes to comfort you, will your sorrow automatically go away? You have heard the fable about the ant and the grasshopper, in which the ant worked hard during the summer while the grasshopper enjoyed idle time. Could the grasshopper understand the ant's experience? The ant worked so hard that his waist became as thin as a thread, and he was exhausted with fatigue. Could the grasshopper comfort the ant if he never had experienced hardship himself? But the father of the ant could understand how the ant felt because the father had worked even harder than his son.

This analogy applies to man and God. God has worked

hard, like the ant, while man has been like the grasshopper. In America people eat, drink, and disco — it's a grasshopper's life. How could such people say they understand God's suffering? Would God be comforted by them? The only way truly to comfort God is to work hard for God's will and understand what He has experienced. Then God might be comforted by you.

Did God begin the universe in joy or sorrow? During the process of creation God felt joy and said that His creation was good, but did He feel the same joy at the human fall? God's joy would have been complete if people had become perfect in the object position, but that never happened. Therefore, human history started in misery, and God's history was also miserable. There was no sound of joyful laughter, only tears. The echo of those tears has resounded throughout history down to the present day.

The sound of tears began history, continued through the centuries, and will be the future agenda of history unless we bring total change. This is the universal atmosphere surrounding our life, so if you are trying to be happy all by yourself it is futile. You are swimming in waters of unhappiness and it is impossible to get out by yourself. Does God have reason to grieve or not? His grief begins in the realization that if things had been different He would have been embraced in joy, but instead He is surrounded by sorrow. Is God's situation clear to humanity?

The Religious Life Is to Comfort God's Grieving Heart

People have restless, unhappy lives, but they don't know why they struggle so much for so little. God knows that bringing a solution to the situation won't be easy. His direction is to bring the solution by following a stony path, but religious people today shun the cross and ask God for blessing and money instead. To God's ears such prayers are worse than seeing the lazy grasshopper-kind of man. Not only do such people not comfort God, but they want to steal something from Him also. Religious people don't realize that they are driving one more nail into God's back each time they pray that way. Instead of comforting Him, it causes Him more pain. On the other hand, if there is a group of people who can say they understand God's situation and who want to take care of His sorrow, will they be closer to God?

Americans like pets, especially puppies. If one day there is a big fight between a husband and wife and the husband throws his wife out of the house, just by licking her hand and wagging his tail the puppy will give her more comfort than her husband. The relationship between humanity and God is somewhat the same. Humanity and God have been in conflict, with people defying God and demanding to know why they should go a stony path. God really needs the comfort of even a little puppy.

Those intellectuals who study God in books will never come close to God without suffering. Maybe they think they have better things to do than to bear the cross, but anyone who thinks in that fashion is a thief. Is the study of books or the way of the cross closer to the heart of God?

If you are trying to be comfortable in a religious life, it cannot work. You have to shed tears; your eyes should not be dry, for there is no such thing as a true religion without tears. You do not know how much I have shed tears in prayer, like the flowing of a stream. You have to cross that creek of tears to meet God. If you shed tears out of self-pity, there is no way God can connect with you, but if you shed tears for humanity and the sorrow of God, He will be linked with you.

God Aspires to True Love

If God exists, what do you think He will be like? What is His goal? Will He run for the United States presidency to show people how powerful He is? Or will He try to become a millionaire like the Rockefellers to show how much money He has? Does God have a hungry stomach and work to get a good meal, or does He merely aspire to have some candy bar from the corner store, like a little child? God must have some aspiration, some goal and ambition. What do you think it is? It is the realization of love. In God's sight, love is the highest and most noble thing.

Where can God find love? Can God love all by Himself and happily laugh and smile and joke with Himself? Will God say, "Here I am. My arms, legs and face are so pleasing to me?" What a crazy idea that is! The person who is trying to be joyful all by himself is ridiculous.

While you women are sitting in front of the mirror making yourself up do you say, "Oh, I'm so pretty. I love myself. My ears and nose are just right!" Are you completely intoxicated by your beauty, or would you rather have someone else praise your beauty? Of course, you wish that someone else would come and say, "Hey, your face is beautiful." Why are you like that? Where does that characteristic desire come from? Do you resemble your parents or friends in that way? No, those are God's traits and characteristics. God cannot sit in front of the mirror admiring Himself.

No matter how big a hand God has, He still wants to

touch the beautiful features of others. He wants to appreciate the beauty coming from His object, not from Himself. God's vision is infinite and He can see through everything in the universe, yet even with that vision, God wants to behold some loved one, no matter how small he may be. God has infinite hearing and He can listen to all the incredible sounds of the universe, yet God aspires to hear the sound of love. God can speak with authority that can create and destroy the universe. His word has that power, yet God wants to use His mouth to whisper love.

God has five senses of sorts. With His spiritual eye He wants to look at the beauty of love; He would like to smell a loving smell; He would like to taste a loving taste; He would like to hear loving voices and loving music; He wants to touch a loving object. That is God's sole aspiration. If God is not that kind of God and His aspiration is only for power or money, what a tasteless God He would be. He would be like an African desert, all vast and powerful but without beauty.

Heaven and Hell

What is the definition of Heaven and hell? Heaven is the place where you become joyful centering upon God, serving Him and dwelling with Him. Hell is where you are sad and empty centering upon Satan. The master of Heaven is God. What is He like? Does He welcome the man who brings money, knowledge or power with him? No, God is looking for something else. Those who are relying on those things will be like pebbles in the Kingdom of Heaven. God is looking for the joy of love, for someone whom He can love and who will bring Him something to be loved.

What is hell? Hell is the place where money and power are valued as ends in themselves and where you yourself become the powerful center. We want to give and receive love so that we can feel joy. Directly opposite to that way of life is hell, where people crush others in order to make themselves kings. Even though someone ends up in hell he doesn't lose the original desire to receive love; that trait will remain even in hell. Even those in hell know what the true aspiration is, and because they cannot achieve it there, they live in agony and torture.

In heaven you yearn for love and you can fulfill it. You can receive God's love and give love to God, over and over without limitation. That is Heaven. Heaven is really wonderful and good, so much so that even if you say thousands of times that it is good you can never truly express how good it is. In Heaven you can live intoxicated in love. When a wave of that love hits you, you are suddenly electrified. A dozing person wakes up and his vision, hearing and sense of smell are sharpened and he will be whispering of the beauty of love for thousands of years. The story of love will never end. Even though every organ of your body is fully active and functioning perfectly, still you feel you want more love. You can become a drunkard of love.

The love God is speaking about and trying to give is profound, infinite love. The love which is worthy of God is not cheap, Hollywood love. Is there any good love in today's world?

Do You Aspire to True Love or to Worldly Love?

I'm sure that in your life you have come to several crossroads and had to make many different choices. You probably took one road and came to a dead-end; then you came back and started on another road but found another dead-end. No matter where you turned in this world, you found no satisfaction, until you tasted God's love. All worldly aspirations pale in comparison. After having tasted that love, you want to become a true person worthy of possessing God's true love forever.

Maybe the best human aspiration is to get a Ph.D. from Harvard? America is the land of opportunity, so why not become a billionaire? Is that your dream, or would you rather become so powerful that everyone has to yield to your wishes? What is your true aspiration? Our goal is the same as God's — true love. How patient can you be until you find the love you are seeking? Is it an easy goal to attain? Can you just sit down and call for love to come to you? Are you searching for cheap love or noble love? Is true love everywhere to be found and easy to have in America today? Can true love be found through casual sex and a series of love affairs in a search for the perfect lover, or in a place like this where we avoid premarital relations and work on changing ourselves into true men and women?

Where is a true man most likely to be found, with rich people or poor people? When you see the structure of our society, do you think the upper, middle or lower class would be more likely to have a true man or true love? Does true love start with crowning glory in the highest place, or in the lowest possible place and then work its way up?

True love comes into being when you practice the highest possible love in the lowest possible place. There you deal with impossible people and try to raise them into the highest possible people by showing them the highest possible standard. There is where true love can be found and can start.

Would you prefer having true love or cheap love? A person who thinks he is clever might prefer taking the easy way. That is why Jesus said that for a rich man to enter the Kingdom of Heaven is far more difficult than for a camel to go through the eye of a needle. Jesus meant that it would be practically impossible, even if the rich man lost all his wealth and sank into poverty. If a poor man could easily enter heaven, why would a rich man never be likely to make it? Once a person becomes self-centered and arrogant, even though he may falter and become penniless he will usually remain self-centered. That quality will not quickly vanish. Poor people, however, have flexibility. Because they have nothing, they are more willing to go anywhere and do anything.

We Meet God in the Place of Tears

Who is true God? God is the One who is searching after His true object to whom He can give true love. God forgets Himself completely and only works for the well-being of the entire creation. Visualize God going after this fallen world. Is He coming with joy, laughing every day and calling "Here is true love. All my fallen children, please come'? Or is He grieving, going after fallen man with tears? Why is the true God the one who is seeking His children with tears?

It is significant that tears come to our eyes on two different occasions—when we are utterly happy and joyful, and when we are utterly sad and sorrowful. God has been crying as a broken-hearted God. When He suddenly finds absolute joy, will He start laughing or keep crying? Imagine lovers who have been separated by war, tearfully searching in hopes of finding each other. They shed tears because of sorrow at having lost each other, but suddenly upon finding each other their tears become tears of joy and they cry even harder.

Then in what circumstances does God want to meet His loved ones? God will meet His loved ones in a tearful place, in a tearful way. If you are absolutely sorrowful and are shaking with sobs then you are not only shedding tears, but fluid is coming from your nose and mouth as well. Have you ever cried in that fashion? If you have never experienced such tears, you have not yet tasted true love. If your expression of tragic sorrow is so deep that it cramps your insides and almost chokes you, in the moment you find your long-lost loved one, what happens? The shock of his return might be so dramatic that you would pass out! That is truly a dramatic encounter. Is that the most dramatic love of all, or is it still not quite at the center of true love?

When you know God's true characteristics do you think He is a God of glory sitting on a throne looking down on the world, happily dispensing His blessings? So far, the Christian world has described this kind of benevolent God, but we in the Unification Church are not looking for such a God. We are seeking the God who is desperately looking for a dramatic encounter with His loved ones. When God is heartbroken and sorrowful and tearfully searching for His family He has no time to think of Himself, and He certainly doesn't worry about His own fame or honor.

God looks very miserable in His search for true love, but that God is truly noble and loving. No one could see God that way and scoff, "What kind of God are you? How can you be so miserable and foolish?" A God of that heart must be praised for giving Himself in an utterly sacrificial way for the sake of His children.

Imagine a loving couple who truly care for each other

unselfishly. If suddenly the wife dies then her husband is completely heartbroken and really cries. If that man happens to be the President of the United States, do you think the citizens will say, "What kind of man are you? As the President how can you show such deep sorrow?" Will people criticize him for showing his genuine grief at the loss of his wife? No. That pure expression of love is a thing to be praised.

We said we are working toward better and higher goals. What are they? The best goal is the desire to be wherever true love can be found. We cannot find true love in the place of glory, however, because God never found it there. We must find it in a tragic situation.

What way of life did Jesus Christ live? He lived the life of the cross and was finally crucified. For whom did he die? Did he die on the cross aspiring to become a Roman emperor or governor of Israel? No, he died gaining salvation for others. All his effort was only to save people. Jesus lived the life of God, desperately seeking His loved ones. Although he gave out his very life for the people, by living in that way he fully occupied God's true love.

Among All Possible Roads, Choose the Road of the Cross

There are many roads meeting at the crossroads. How can we distinguish whether a certain road is wrong and not leading to the ultimate goal? We look at every road from the point of view of true love. If true love doesn't come alive on a particular road, you won't find any satisfaction and you will know it is the wrong direction.

If a child is drowning, a parent jumps into the water to save his child and will even die in his place. What kind of love is that? It is sacrificial, true love. Suppose a friend is drowning and another friend saves him and dies in his place. What kind of friend is that? Of course, he is a true friend. Is this the same on the national level? If America is sacrificial in trying to save a small nation such as Vietnam, does the same theory apply? Did America meet the standard?

Where is the Unification Church? Established churches have lots of money, honor and fame, but all of a sudden the Unification Church has emerged and challenged them all, saying, "We want to go in a completely different direction." Usually churches take a collection at service on Sunday mornings and a devout Christian tithes one tenth of his income, keeping his home and whatever extra money he needs. We don't have any extra money, however. We go out to raise money, giving our blood, sweat and labor to save the world. Just like Jesus, we want to give ourselves to save the world, and in the process we are willing to sacrifice and die. We know how to live comfortably like anyone else, but we gave up that life. We are here to sacrifice. We live the simplest way of life and eat humble meals. We don't spend money but work hard, and the fruit of that labor is given for the sake of the world.

You know how to live well and eat well. We all know how to wallow in luxury. Let the world live that way. We don't do it, because we are willing to sacrifice for the sake of the world. We embrace the sacrificial way of life that was established by Jesus. We are the people who forget ourselves and cry out for others, praying for heaven to bless them. We want to be in the position to give ourselves up for that purpose. We choose that way of life.

Our life style is parallel to Jesus' life. Therefore, we

can evoke such heartfelt passion in the heart of God. As I said, God is coming down to humanity in a tearful, heartbroken way. If you go this way, then the moment He meets you is the moment He truly has hope, comfort and encouragement. God came all the way down and has finally found people who understand Him. Here He has true comrades and champions, and God feels comforted. We want to give God a shock of joy. When He meets you, let Him find someone who suffers and is more sorrowful than Himself. Then He will be comforted. God will want to champion you and comfort you and will no longer be sad. Let us surprise Him by comforting His heart.

Repentance on the Road

Do you pray? How do you pray? If your prayer is centered mostly on personal requests, it is neither valuable nor powerful. When you are too self-centered and only want individual advancement, God just cannot listen to that prayer. The first thing is to determine a righteous direction and to work toward the goal, repenting in daily religious life. God will always listen to the needs of such a person. Actually, ninety percent of prayer is not about doing this or that, because you and God already know what must be done; ninety percent of prayer is repentance. This parallels Jesus' teaching to repent, for the Kingdom of Heaven is at hand. Repentance is very valuable if you do it correctly.

Since your goal is already set very high, you always know on which days you don't reach it. Repent on those days, saying, "God, I'm sorry about today. I really wanted to come much closer to the goal today but I failed you. Please forgive me. I will do it tomorrow." That's the way you should pray.

Some day you may be witnessing when some big guy strides up to harass you, yanking your necktie and shouting, "You stupid Moonie." At that moment perhaps you can't stand the difficulty any more and you snap, "Yes, I'm a Moonie. So what?" Then you come back and pray, "God, I'm sorry. That was not Your expectation. You want me to do better than that, don't You?"

The next day may find you having to repent again. When you set your goal very high you cannot reach it easily, and every day you repent. That's a beautiful thing. Every day is a new day and a new beginning. You have a lifelong journey and every day is a day of repentance. That's a beautiful life to live. That is far better than feeling, "Now I'm the leader, and I give the directions around here." The other way is a far more beautiful way of life.

God has never boasted, "I'm Almighty God so you have to listen to Me." Then how could we who are trying to comfort that heartbroken God say that we are somebody? We have not come that far yet. The person who repents every day makes progress, even without knowing it. Anyone who thinks he is a high-standard Moonie and a good example for others has already stopped growing. Would you like to go the road of repentance?

I want you to realize that even after lifelong repentance no one will have paid his debt. On the road of repentance every day is a new beginning. That is the road of your very own cross, on which you are going only upwards and will never fall down. Many times Jesus secluded himself in the mountains, fasting and praying tearfully. Even for him, every day was a new day of repentance. That's the one sure way you can guarantee you will make progress and never falter.

Today my topic concerns the crossroad of life and death. What road do we take? We can choose many, but let's take only one — the road of the cross.

The Road of America is Leading to Hell

Another way is the road of selfishness. There is a road for the benefit of your home and another for your country. American citizens can be classified into three categories: those who live for themselves, those who live for the well-being of their own family, and those patriots who are trying to advance the cause of the nation. Where do the majority of Americans belong? Maybe more than ninety percent are self-centered. Who is going to be responsible for the homes and nation of such people?

The road of unselfishness is God's road, and you can reach Him only by going in this direction. Because of self-centeredness there is a barrier between God and America. Can Americans find God? Then is this nation the Kingdom of Heaven or hell? The logical conclusion is that ninety percent of Americans are living in hell. The fact is that Americans today are proud of their civilization, but do you know what kind of civilization you have? It is a jungle which is seething with all kinds of criminality and immorality. We are desperately trying to get out of that jungle. Everyone's mind has been contaminated there, to the point where they sometimes feel very comfortable and accustom to living even in such a wretched jungle.

Where do you want to live, here in America or in Africa? Africa may have a physical jungle, but perhaps Africans live very simple and unselfish lives, thinking more about their own families and tribes and nation than about themselves. If that is the case, do you think it is better or worse than America? If it is better, then naturally you would want to live in Africa.

You have been programmed by a contaminated world and become accustomed to it. Selfishness is everywhere —in the homes, nations and even religions. Even religion has not survived in purity. America was founded by people of great faith, but most of today's churches are broken down. America had strong families who built a righteous nation, but all that is breaking down. If the nation is crumbling, what is its destiny? The ultimate consequence can only be destruction and despair, and there will be no hopeful future left. If America continues on this path, then not only this nation but the rest of the world will crumble. Furthermore, by continuing this way of life, America will make God's work fail. America is going over the cliff, and someone must come to apply the brakes and stop it.

We are the ones whom God has called to apply the brakes. We must revitalize this country's mainstay, which is religion, and give it a new tradition. We are confronting a great tidal wave, but we will push it back. This nation has been pursuing an abnormal way, so we are here to apply the brakes and turn it around 180 degrees.

This is the crossroad of life and death. The road of life is really the way of death, while the road of death is really the way of life. It is practically impossible to change a place of death into a place of life, and merely surviving requires a desperate struggle, but we will not give up or die. We will suffer and overcome death and turn it into life.

The Road to God Requires Self-Denial

Who here has experienced tears during prayer? Which kind of tears did you shed—sad tears because you were tired and felt you couldn't go on? Have you shed tears for God? How do you know God has shed tears? Your experience with God has been indirect. How can you relate to God? How can you change and be linked directly to God?

In relation to God the key word is Father. Even at the time of Adam and Eve God was invisible, but Adam and Eve were created to be the visible form of God. They were like the body of God, and God was like their mind. In spirit world as well Adam and Eve would have been the visible form of God. God created man and woman so He could manifest Himself in a visible form; He wanted to have a visible form to communicate with. Second, God created man and woman to fulfill love. God is our Father. Human beings are temples of God, and inside the temple dwells a mind which is a microcosm of the infinite God.

How far is God from you? He is as near as your mind, for that is His dwelling place. God knows good and evil, and your mind also knows what is good and what is evil. Your mind knows whether you are headed for Heaven or hell. Your mind is a proper guide, but the problem is whether your mind is strong enough to pull your body toward the goal. If the body fails to obey then you go to hell. You resemble this infinite God because you possess all the elements of that God. In order to be His child you must be like Him.

All of history hinges upon one word — restoration — because Adam and Eve never became God's dwelling place. Right now, your body is always pulled in the satanic direction, so your mind has to be anchored to God and be able to conquer your body. Your little mind must become big in order to do that job. Right now there is a race between the two, and when your mind overwhelms your body there is no chance your body can go astray. The person who can discipline his body most will grow fastest. You have to make it a habit to subjugate your body to your mind, a process that takes about three to seven years.

Therefore, you should do whatever your body dislikes. Since the body always goes in a satanic direction, you should do whatever it doesn't want to do. This is why we do many things our bodies don't like. Our bodies don't like to fund-raise or fast or witness, but that's what we do.

America has a very promiscuous society in which men and women have a free lifestyle and can do anything. In this society full of temptations you must keep yourselves pure. That one effort alone is like a life-and-death struggle. By the age of thirty most Americans may have been married three or four times, but you are withstanding temptation and sustaining your purity up to that age. In the everyday world you can make a girlfriend in one night; with an absolute stranger you can do all kinds of crazy things overnight. But here even husbands and wives sometimes have few opportunities to be together. This kind of discipline takes a drastic effort, and you feel that you are practically dying, but I want you to know that you are truly living for eternity.

Do you go the flat path or the stony path? Have you ever imagined how rugged the stony path is? You women want to marry handsome, elegant men, don't you? You are so silent all of a sudden! Your eyes are cunning in a way because they recognize when a man is handsome and tall, and then you hope he might become your husband. But you must deny what your eyes see and what your body wants. Ask God for the ugliest possible man so that you can look at him as being in the image of God and serve him. People always say, "Yes, yes, yes," except for one thing. That "except" is always the problem.

It is my experience that God is the champion at disguising Himself. He tries to give you the utmost love, but in order to ensure that you are qualified for it He will disguise that love in the form of the ugliest person. When you truly love that person as you love God and give God your thanks, then God will slowly reveal Himself through that person. There is always temptation behind a beautiful face, so watch out. Goodness dwells behind the ugly facade, and furthermore, no one will look at that person except you!

Some of you may think I say this because I already have a beautiful wife. But actually I really asked God to give me the ugliest, woman in the world. I was totally ready to receive a 250-pound wife because I thought God might want me to appreciate His bigness. If you have a small wife, then you can think God wants you to enjoy His charming side.

Can you overcome what your eyes tell you? You weren't given eyes so you could look at the world in a secular way, but so you could shed God's tears. That's the most precious way to use your two eyes. You like to hear sweet words, don't you? You have to cross over the hill of your ears also. Maybe your husband is not only ugly, but every day he grumbles and complains. What would you say? In order to separate your thoughts from Satan, you have to think that the grumbling is sweet music from God. When your husband keeps snapping and nagging, give him his breakfast and tell him to nag afterward. At night, tell him to sleep and then nag tomorrow. Do that for forty days, and then he will say it is no fun nagging because there is no response from you.

Your nose is very sensitive. Everyone likes and dislikes certain smells, but you should train yourselves to like unpleasant odors — such as a toilet smell, or your husband's body odor. Overcome the hill of all your senses. How many exams have you passed? You can always come up with excuses. Some people might say they can't get up early because their hips are too small and they don't have strength in their back. Another person might say her hips are so big she can't carry them early in the morning! Your body always makes excuses.

Your hand knows what your body wants, so your hands reach for the nicest food before anyone else gets it. You should tell your hand to reach for the things other people don't like. A woman's body offers a certain temptation and has a certain craving to be touched, and so women have to cross the hill of hips and bosom. Men also have their own hill to cross. You have to transcend temptation and not do what your body wants.

There are seven tests to go over — eyes, ears, mouth, hands, nose, legs, bosom and hips. Keep a list and cross off each test as you pass it. But denying temptation is only the beginning. Then you must utilize all these organs to cry out in understanding God. Have you experienced having not only tears running down your face, but saliva drooling and your nose running as you cry in prayer? If someone tries to talk to you at that time, you don't hear them, and if they touch you, you don't feel it. Furthermore, with that heart you want to shed every drop of blood for the people. God wants to see your whole body dripping sweat as it works for humanity.

I Have Lived to Liberate God from His Tears

God has been shedding tears all these years, not for Himself but for humanity and the world. Therefore, we shed tears for God and humanity, not for ourselves. The secular world sheds tears, but heavenly tears should be greater than those tears. Knowing that the dispensational path had to be walked, I never cried for myself, or for my family and parents. I cried for God and humanity. My tears soaked all my clothes, even my thick winter clothes.

That's the only way I could inherit God's kingdom and lay the foundation for the Unification Church. Those tears are the root of the Unification Church. I would like to change the tears of people sorrowful for themselves into heavenly tears shed for God's circumstances. Neighbors and brothers tried to kill me by sentencing me to a prison where prisoners were worked and starved to death slowly. But I shed tears and overcame death. Even in prison I never complained. I never begged God to ease my pain. My only worry was that my blood and sweat were shed for God's sake.

My path has been nothing but a way of misery, many tears and much hardship. Do you think I am insensitive or dumb? Any time I take a beating or see some sorrow, I must shed tears for God. When those situations come to me I always think of God first, that I am the person to liberate Him. Then I cannot help but comfort Him and tell Him I am fine. I know also that God has shed many tears because of me, and that is why He cannot forget the Unification Church.

People who communicate with the spirit world sometimes ask to know about me, and the answer comes to them in the form of desperate crying for days and nights. I cannot be described without tears. If you are without tears in the Unification Church, you cannot successfully go this way. I cannot feel close to people who do not know the taste of tears. Only those people who know tears can understand me.

Fallen humanity has been burdened by a debt of blood, sweat and tears. If you ask God to tell you some of His experiences since the fall, there is nothing else He can tell except a story of sweat and tears and blood. He has no other history but that. Today's Christians truly don't know what God is all about. They imagine Him sitting on a glorious throne enjoying life, but that is not true at all.

Someone has to liberate God, and He cannot do it Himself. The agony of parents, or of husband and wife, cannot be solved by themselves alone. The agony of parents can only be solved by children; the agony of a husband can only be solved by his wife, and the agony of a wife by her husband. The only way to liberate God from His sorrow is by becoming a son of filial piety to take over His agony, or by becoming like a wife who takes over the agony of her husband.

Even if you are not the children of certain parents, or the wife of a certain man, if you serve those people more than their actual children or wife do, you will actually be closer to them than their own family. The only way to help is to show more filial piety and genuine devotion than their own children or wife would do. The same truth applies to our relationship with God. If you give more sacrificial love to God than I do, you will be closer to Him than I am. I suffered all my life for God, but if anyone of you can do better then certainly God will be closer to you. If God loves you more, will I be jealous at how you are doing better than I am? No, I will be happy to follow such people.

God wants to be with anybody who has such love. If you shed your sweat, tears and blood all your life for God, then because of you God will be able to shed tears of happiness and hope for the first time. What other honor could you ask for? You won't have to worry about going to heaven; God Himself will personally escort you to the highest place. The greatest path in history is the path of liberating God from His sorrow.

A true son of filial piety will move his parents' heart to tears. The true loyal subject will move his king to tears. If many subjects can give their lives for their king and queen, they will certainly be moved to tears. That is my goal — I am giving all my devotion to the task of liberating God from tears of sorrow and moving Him to shed tears of happiness. That is the root of the Unification Church.

Our Tears Will Restore the Tears of History

Adam shed tears, Cain and Abel shed blood, Seth shed tears, and they all passed these tears down to history. In order to make restitution, Noah shed sweat, blood and tears for 120 years in truly sacrificial devotion. That's why God can use that faith to wipe out the world of tears, sweat and blood. When Abraham left his home he shed tears; his son Isaac was offered to be a sacrifice, conditionally shedding blood; his grandson Jacob really shed sweat. This is the pattern of pioneering the dispensation.

Moses was thrown out of the Pharaoh's palace, and many times he shed tears. Jesus shed blood on the cross. The Lord of the Second Advent will shed the most sweat in finally building the Kingdom. It was sown at the time of Adam and Eve, and is reaped in this way throughout history.

Someone must liquidate the sorrowful blood, sorrowful sweat, and sorrowful tears of history, and then build a new history of joy in laboring for the Kingdom. At the time of the Lord of the Second Advent restitution must be made totally; therefore, the Lord must be a king of sweat, tears and blood, paying the debt of all history.

In the midst of tears, can you harbor hope for Heaven? Jesus bore the cross at the age of 33. Our determination is to bear the cross, but to bear a living cross instead. For whom will you do it, though? For God and humanity. With tears of sorrow Adam and Eve brought the fall and brought the tears and tragedy which humanity has suffered for many thousands of years, but tears for God and humanity will not only bring you up to heaven, they will also liberate God.

We shall overcome the stony path of death and find life. This is why Jesus said that he who would save his life would lose it, and he who would give his life would save it. When we cross over that path of tears and the people of the world can shed tears of happiness, God will finally be able to shed tears of happiness. God is looking at this room, with five colors of skin gathered in one common love, for one common goal, shedding tears of joy and hope as parents and children, and that scene brings God tears of joy and hope.

God bless you. Let us pray.

6
THE FORMULA FOR WORLD PEACE

The primary question facing humankind is that of peace. The democratic world has no direction, and we who know the heart and will of God must guide it. No one knows what will be the end result of the powerful, enormous communist world. Furthermore, when we talk about the destiny of the world, we are not talking about one hundred or one thousand years in the future, but about today. The world situation is deteriorating so rapidly that sometimes I am fearful about whether we can turn the situation around.

Conflicts and Wars Are Endemic in This World

For all of us to be happy it is logical that there should be no wars and conflicts and antagonism between people. Certainly we can say that war is not good unless the fighting can be for the benefit of the whole. In war it is unlikely that one victor will completely annihilate the enemy. There are bound to be some men left alive on

133

the opposing side, and it is predictable that, until they dissipate the antagonism in their hearts, they will stick together and somehow try to get revenge. If the victorious country becomes weak, the people who had lost the war will look for some opportunity to retaliate. The result is a vicious cycle in which the losing side from one war concentrates on becoming strong enough to dominate its former conquerors.

Today the democratic world and the communist world are both seeking global dominion, but which side is putting more effort into conquering the world? It's very simple to say that the stronger will win over the weaker, and in this case it means that the communist world must be victorious for it is making the greater effort. The world is facing a very dangerous age, and if there existed no God and no spirit world then the world would already be doomed.

Suppose America were to defeat the Soviet Union. Assuming some people survive the struggle, would they attain lasting peace? When the cause is wrong, the effect is always wrong. The effect cannot be changed without changing the cause. Human history so far has been sown in blood and war, so we can only reap such an effect. Therefore, to obtain a new effect in history we have to begin with a new cause, with a fertile land to receive the seeds of peace.

But today, such a godly nation which could become the basis for a peaceful world does not exist. All the fatherlands which people claim have no connection with God. All the characteristics of the different nations resulted from division in the world, usually coming out of war and struggle. That's the way new nations are born. There are many boundaries on earth, all of which are stained by the blood of soldiers killed in hostilities.

The highest wall built to prevent invasion is the one you build between you and your neighbor. As technology advances we can travel to the other side of the world in a short time, but nations continue to struggle with their neighbors as they did in ancient times. National boundaries have always been stained by the blood of their people. For all the hundreds of nations on earth there have been thousands of struggles throughout history, resulting in many divisions of sovereignty. That happened because of the human fall and humanity's separation from God. What do we mean when we say the human fall? It means that humans and God became enemies instead of being one, and that there has been struggle instead of harmony and peace between humans and God.

Does the Communist Dialectic Explain Conflict in the World?

If a person does not have religious experience or understanding, he thinks that humans were created to live in this state of conflict. Some scholars conclude that God cannot be perfect, that He created humankind to live this way and improve little by little every day. If God is good, how can He put up with so much evil and corruption in the world? No one can look at the wonder of this vast, infinite universe and not sense that there is some awesome power behind it. But at the same time, when a person looks at the corruption of human society, it is common that he will doubt the existence of God. The fact of conflict and struggle appears to be real, while the idea of an omnipotent, loving God appears to be an illusion.

Karl Marx was confused about God in this way. He felt a contradiction within himself, between his childhood faith in God and the questions he had in his mind. His theory of dialectics, which is based upon the importance of conflict and struggle, arose from within his own mind and his experience of conflict. He could not accept the existence of God, given the reality of so much conflict and struggle in the world. He proclaimed that for him, history and material were "god." Communism or Marxism is an ideology which strives to explain the universe on an atheistic basis.

The communist theory contends that there are always two elements in conflict with each other. If we apply this to the communists themselves, then once no other element outside their ideology exists in the world, where would the conflict be? Marxism predicts that history will go beyond the socialistic age, and after that the communistic utopia will arrive, but we are forced to ask the communists what the objective of their struggle would be then.

Since dialectical materialism maintains that progress results only from struggle and that without struggle nothing will grow, we can ask what would happen when the whole world comes under communism. How would the communists go on living? Will they go on fighting among themselves to maintain progress in their own world, or will they sit still and do nothing? Can there ever be a peaceful communist world? According to their own theory that cannot be. When everything reaches a climax and there is no more growth, they will have to start fighting among themselves.

Every person has within himself some fervor for an ideal. Working on the basis of the framework of contradiction, communism tries to solve the problems of the world. However, it only looks at the problems externally. Because communists deny God and proclaim materialism. Religion, on the other hand, recognizes the same contradictions but digs deeper into the situation. Human history is undeniably a history of struggle and conflict, so communists believe that progress can only be gained through the same process — struggle and conflict. But the true cause of all the struggles has not been revealed to them; its elucidation is the responsibility of religion.

When you dig down deeper and deeper, you will hit the core where true peace and true love prevail; however that core has not yet been widely explained. America is a nation founded upon the Christian philosophy. But Americans have not yet dug down to the very depths and core of Christianity; they have not yet found the foundation. A purely external viewpoint promotes individualism and division, while an internal viewpoint promotes the well-being of the whole and unification. Thus the two are contradictory viewpoints.

I am not denying the rights of individuals or the fact that valid divisions exist in the world. I am simply saying that the largest purpose and unification come first and upon that foundation everything external can be fulfilled as well. Within the family, a man and woman come together to create one whole, common purpose and they create some form of unity. Only then do they go out and do their individual activities; but first they must create the structure of a common purpose within the family. When the whole purpose is placed in the subjective position and the individual purpose in the objective, both can be fulfilled. But if you try to reverse that order, everything is destroyed.

An important question is, if God exists why do such divisions and conflicts exist? We can answer by explaining the human fall. Because of the fall, people's internal life was destroyed and only their external life was able to flourish. God had to devise some method by which to restore the world, so He inspired the development of the different religions throughout history. The one simple sign of God's existence is that there are major religions all over the world.

Yet those who observe the incapacity of religious groups to solve world problems conclude that God must not exist. Even Christians are so confused that they seriously consider the possibility of a Christian communism. If we have clear minds, can we possibly say that such a thing as Christian Marxism or an atheistic clergy can exist? Can religious people solve the world's problems by ignoring the reality of God and embracing Marxism? Religion today is so discredited that people freely adapt it at their convenience to better their way of life. Religion is not fulfilling its original mission nowadays.

Love Your Enemy—The Solution to World Peace

Today the world is filled with more hatred than love between neighbors. There is division between individuals, between nations, even between religions. Unless we can start with a new beginning, a new world cannot come about. Human history started from lies, so we have to re-start human history from truth. Unless a new movement develops which can sow true peace, there will be no lasting peace.

If there is an Almighty God, would He be content to put up with today's reality, or would He do something to change the world back into its original shape? If there is someone here on earth commissioned by God to take over His mission and cause, what would that man or group claim? He would proclaim that the world's present course is in error, insisting that humankind must turn around. He must tell humankind that their direction must be entirely changed.

What would be the slogan of that man? If you are clever you should be able to figure that out. If the world began in hatred and lies, then a course which is 180 degrees different would be one of absolute love, love so great that you love even your own enemy. To me that is a powerful slogan which can change the course of history. Can you find anything more powerful than this? Some might think that that is an easy answer, but when you don't know what it is it seems very difficult to find. All the saints of history have searched for this answer.

If you have such great love that you can love even your enemy, that power will melt everything. God needs churches that can melt the wrong world down and change it into the right one. The entire world of religion is pursuing this one slogan, though in varying degrees. Which of all the saints do you think God would love the most? The answer is simple because there is someone who proclaimed this slogan forcefully. Jesus Christ stands like a giant because this proclamation was the hallmark of his life.

We all want to live in an ideal society, but in reality we are living in a chaotic, confused, fallen society. This is our problem. How can we bring all this confusion under control? Could we make things better if we had the absolute power of tyranny? That's what the communists have tried to do. They try to rule with an iron fist, and they seem to succeed, at first. They have conquered nations and taken over governments, but eventually the communists will fall.

Recently Soviet Russia suffered a great drought. Certainly the heads of state didn't want that drought to occur. They may have cried out with clenched fists, "We have the power in this country! Give us rain!" But that is not the way nature operates. God judged them by holding back the rain for three years. Even if you have enough power to make the nation tremble, you cannot bring about the ideal society. Likewise, knowledge alone cannot bring the solution. Money is not the way either.

The ultimate tool by which to bring about the ideal society is love, true love. What is this true love? If we say God-centered love, what exactly do we mean? The best definition was given by Jesus: true, God-centered love is that which is capable of loving even an enemy. If white people love other white people, there's nothing special about that. When white people love black people, though, that is true love. But the ultimate love is that of loving our enemy. That is the ultimate love because no one can criticize or condemn such love. It is invincible love, love which is always there, without contradiction, always smoothly flowing.

Does America Live Up to This Standard?

What are the qualities of a saint? A saint loves all of humanity as his own family, his own country. This standard never changes throughout history. How many people have lived and practiced such a way of life? How many saints are there in America? Wherever you travel in the world there are anti-American movements. Americans are hated and are even expelled from many places in the world. Why? Because few Americans have been living according to this principle. Mostly they have been trying to benefit themselves at the expense of the world. In general they have not tried to help or serve any country except the United States.

Many times Americans do not try to teach their technology to other countries but just keep it to themselves as a secret. But people with true love would see that this is not the right kind of ethical practice. This kind of standard has to be criticized and condemned in the name of justice. True love would go in the opposite direction.

America, for example, has given foreign aid to certain countries. Instead of expecting a return on that money, as though it were an investment, America ought to give that money and forget it. She should let the money work for the good of the local inhabitants. What if parents kept a record of how much money they spent on each child, saying, "Last year I spent $5,000 on you, so you owe me $5,000. For the last thirty years, you owe me $45,000." Is that the parental way? Of course not. Parents do everything unconditionally for the children, and forget what they have done.

I want to see you become men and women who can go beyond your country and love mankind everywhere as much as you love the people of your own country— in fact, even more than you love your own country. That is the Unification goal.

Why do I have to come to America, a country which does not even give me a decent welcome? Because America is vitally important to God and to the future peace of the world. America must go out to the world, the six continents and five races of the earth, and give of herself and her wealth. Four billion people are waiting for the touch of America's hand. You must go out and serve them.

If America succeeds in this mission, then the glory and prosperity of this nation will have no end. But if she insists on keeping her wealth for herself, then it is a natural consequence that America will one day fall from her fortunate position. Love is the key. It is love alone that will connect all things together and bring them to

the altar of God. When America offers her wealth to the
world, God will turn around and give it all back to her
as His blessing. That will mark the beginning of the
Kingdom of God on earth.

Instead of bothering to work in America, I could have
said, "Forget it. I don't want to bother with the United
States." But that is not my way of life. The more this
country comes against me, the more I will work to melt
the opposition with an intense love. Even the communists
are trying to kill me, but I am trying to warm them up
with my love and ultimately restore them. That is my
philosophy and it is one which will go on without di-
minishing for all eternity.

Loving One's Enemies Can
Reconcile Warring Nations

My entire life has been one of persecution and mistreatment. Yet you see that I am not tired. I keep moving,
step by step, leaving footprints as I go. When I turn
around I can taste a precious joy at seeing them behind
me. Up ahead there is nothing but persecution coming
at me, like a headwind pushing against me. But I feel
great exaltation when I turn around and look behind me,
and I see people of all races following me. I see peace,
harmony and unity. That is so beautiful and valuable to
me that I then can move ahead even more strongly.

Consider the Japanese people and the Korean people.
They were enemies for quite a long time. But today, the
Japanese members are pledging their service and loyalty
under me, a Korean man. They are even willing to marry
Korean spouses. Isn't that amazing? They are not pledging their lives for the sake of Rev. Moon; not at all. They
are pledging their lives for the sake of the true love which

I pioneered and championed. In this way, the enemy nations of Japan and Korea are being reconciled.

When Jesus was on earth there was a wall of hatred between the great Roman Empire and the little nation of Israel because one was conqueror and the other the conquered. Jesus knew that the only way to conquer Rome was through love. Rome conquered Israel with military power, but Israel could conquer Rome through love. Even though Jesus was crucified, he could still pray for God to forgive the very people who killed him. No power could be any greater. Love can overcome any walls, no matter how high and thick. Jesus knew that individuals have enemies, families have enemies, and tribes and nations have enemies. Hatred and animosity always cause killing on each level, and only one strategy can break down this wall — love your enemy.

The fallen world always responds to animosity by seeking revenge. If God and Jesus had used the method of revenge, however, then there would not be one human being left here on earth because God would have extinguished them all in retribution. A great movement of restoration only comes from this ideology of love. Only the power of love could begin the new history and new age. When a person has the power to love even his enemies, he is truly a giant and there is nothing he cannot deal with or embrace. Ultimately that person shall conquer the world in God's way. Christianity has always possessed that ideology, and God sees that as long as Christians pursue that doctrine then they shall conquer.

A New Christian Movement Is Needed to Save the World

When you plant bean seeds, beans will grow. When you plant carnations, carnations will grow. No one can deny this principle. If you sow hatred, hatred will result. When you sow love, then the fruit of love will indeed come. The important thing is the size of that love. Christianity has been failing to live up to this principle and failing to love its enemies. This has been its major difficulty.

Christians preach about loving one's enemies, but Jesus also said to love your neighbor. Who is a Christian's neighbor? Certainly it is another Christian. But are they doing it? Do Catholics love Mormons? Do Jehovah's Witnesses love Methodists? It doesn't matter who calls us heretics; whoever practices this principle of loving one's enemy is closer to God and is the orthodox Christian. That is my belief. Love can unite. If Christians practice love, then Christians can unite with other Christians and then Christians can unite all the religions of the world.

Aren't we heretics? Why not? How do you know? When we tell other Christians what the Unification Church is about, many will say we are heretics. The important thing is to inherit the true tradition and spirit of Christianity, however, and as long as we inherit that doctrine and practice it, we are the most orthodox.

God loves the world, and that is why He made such a great investment in Christianity, but now decline is setting in. Even though the leaders of world Christianity are aware of this, they don't know how to retrieve the situation. The degree of decline is so severe that even though people search for God and believe in Jesus as their Savior, God's Spirit is no longer found in many churches at this time. The great theological question is: after God raised up this great Christian foundation, why can't we find much of the former spirit remaining?

Let's take an example from an orchard. If the orchard's

owner sees that all the trees are in trouble, He undertakes a pruning process in order to save them. Once God concluded that Christianity was not up to the task of saving the entire world, he has to restore the churches by cutting away the sick branches to encourage the healthy ones. The owner of the orchard will not favor the old branches, but will encourage the new buds and branches and leaves.

To save the whole world it is logical from God's point of view that He must prune Christendom because it had become ineffective. God needs a new Christian movement that will have the mission of saving the whole orchard. What kind of Christian movement will He use to revive declining Christianity? It should have the purpose and content to overcome the four major problems: conflict among nations, division among Christian denominations, conflict between races, and conflict between the religions of the world.

There is much division among nations because people are egocentric. From God's point of view, He is not really God of this earth. He sees that all nations originated within an environment of immorality, conflict and disharmony, and have nothing to do with Him. The new religious movement which God is seeking should have the content that will enable it to solve the problems of conflict among the nations.

Why are there so many Christian denominations when Christians all claim one Savior? They split apart because each denomination insisted on its own theory and logic. All of these churches are false when compared to the one true body which Christianity should be. This is a second great problem to solve.

The third problem is finding a worldwide solution for the division of races. We can predict that a final showdown must come between blacks and whites and other races as their relations worsen. War is the inevitable outcome unless a religious solution is found. Ideological and philosophical solutions will only further divide the races because each ideology will insist on its own solution. At this moment communism is actually trying to promote division and conflict between the races.

Soon, not only racial conflict but also conflict between the different religions will begin to appear. Hinduism and Buddhism influence primarily the Oriental peoples, while Islam is dominant among the Arabs, and so forth. There is a possibility of collision between these world religions. Communist strategy for the future is to take a more active role in weakening religion, generating conflict among Islam, Christianity, Judaism and other faiths. Through promoting division among peoples and religions, the communists want to further their own purposes.

God's new religious movement should have the content which can unite not only these diverse religions but even draw together people who follow the different ideologies, such as communism and democracy. If God does exist then He would reason this way, but He also needs someone on earth to carry out this thinking.

Love Will Overcome the World's Problems

A diagnosis needs to be made of the world's problem, the nation's problem, religion's problem, the racial problem, the ideological problem, and the family's problem. All levels of society need a spiritual doctor.

All these problems started when humankind went in the wrong direction in the beginning. From that time everything has been going in a direction opposite to God's point of view. How can we turn the right side to the left side and vice versa? We have to go against the old, established desires. The whole problem is one of changing the direction of the "I"-centered family, the "I"-centered nation and "I"-centered religion and world. We have to go the opposite way and live the family life for the nation, the national life for the world and dedicate the world to God. The present way of living in the world must be completely turned upside down. "I" must live for the world, not for "my" sake. Judaism should exist for Islam and Islam for Judaism. Christianity should live for Buddhism and so forth. This is what is meant by the opposite direction.

Without going opposite its present direction there is no chance for the world to go in God's direction. Selfish instinct prevails instead of a striving to love one another. Yet, the formula of loving one another really works. When this is applied, it will turn the world upside down.

My philosophy is very simple. If you have the attitude to love your enemy, then you can overcome any situation and there is no obstacle that can block you. In my lifetime of sixty years there were many things I didn't want to tackle, but I did them because I loved my enemy. I did the worst things there were to do — I was a beggar, a laborer, a farmer, a fisherman, a dockworker, a miner. Every day I am living this principle, and when I look I see that there are many people of all colors following behind me. The Unification Church principle is rather simple and we live it. From the moment you can love your enemy, the Kingdom of Heaven shall come. God doesn't only want individuals to love their enemies. He wants to see an entire nation that will practice this principle.

We are multi-colored here; this auditorium is a miniature of the heavenly Kingdom, with five colors of skin from 127 countries. All we have to do is practice this principle. We are not going to destroy our enemies but liberate them. We find love by loving them. Practice this in your daily life. That is where you can learn to bear the burden and taste God's tears and broken heart.

Let us pray.

7

THE HEART
OF REUNION

I am very happy to see all of you again after being away for 70 days. When you are separated from someone, you long for them the most if you share a common purpose or goal. Then you both yearn to see each other and look forward to the day of reunion. I am Korean and you are Americans and we come from the opposite ends of the world. There must be a providential purpose linking the two extremes of East and West; otherwise you would not miss me and I would not miss you and we would not look forward to meeting each other again.

To the ordinary person it may seem as if the vast ocean is one stationary body of water. Actually the ocean is continually in motion, with cold currents and warm currents running their separate courses and colliding at certain points. All kinds of movement can be found in the ocean. The tides come in and go out twice a day and tidal flows all over the globe are linked together. Beneath the ocean's surface there is a great variety of fish, which are influenced by the currents and the tidal waters. Often many fish gather where the warm and cold currents collide creating certain areas famous for fishing such as the Georges Bank off the coast near Boston. Different types of fish live in fresh or salt water, but at spawning time certain species go to an estuary, where the fresh and salt water flow together, to lay their eggs.

It is very intriguing and even mystical to see how the places and times of meeting and coming together are very important in all forms of life. For instance, the ancient cultures such as developed in Greece and Rome without exception began to grow at places where land and water meet. No early human civilization could prosper apart from a river or the sea.

The Harmony of Extremes

When the distance between two parts is extreme, there is always greater joy, emotion and drama involved in their reunion than if they had not experienced such extreme separation. I came from a land on the other side of the globe, a land that many Americans think of as being a remote country. In their minds they still envision Korea as being ravaged by war. It is as if the U.S. were on the pinnacle of a mountain while Korea was in the depths of a valley. That is why many people cannot understand how a man from Korea can attract such attention in a nation which stands at the pinnacle of modern-day culture.

In the vast ocean a tremendous variety of things happen when the warm and cold currents meet. When the five races gather together we are like five kinds of ocean current flowing into the same area, and extraordinary things can happen as a result. It is not my will or your will but some providential will that makes this so. There must be a universal power that pushes two extremes to unite for a greater purpose.

Exciting music is not made with just one or two tones, but with tones that range from high to low and with a variety of instruments. That blending of extremes makes exciting music. At the same time, one instrument alone cannot create excitement. In order to make the drums exciting the drummer has to combine many motions and gestures as well as rhythms. The violin combines different extremes, using thin strings to create very feminine, beautiful sounds. The beauty of the violin is that even though it has only a few strings, it is possible to produce extreme variation in sound.

The union of people from East and West can be compared to playing the violin: Westerners are like the low notes of a violin while Asians are like the high notes. Americans walk with a long, swinging stride, but the Japanese walk lightly, taking small steps. More excitement is created when the two extremes unite to make one harmonized picture. We do not use the word harmony to describe primarily the unity of similar things. The most moving, beautiful harmony is created when extremes come together. The value of harmony lies in this unity and diversity.

What color flowers do you like? Everyone has a different preference. If everyone liked only the color yellow, then everything in the entire world would soon be yellow, with yellow clothes and even yellow lipstick. The result would be a mad, mad world of yellow! The blending together of all kinds of colors can be interpreted and understood in many different ways; it is a universal mystery. When you can see your feelings reflected in different ways, you never tire of such beauty. Would everyone without exception like to have blue eyes? How about having a blue tongue or blue skin and teeth? Why did God give blue eyes to some people? The people who have white skin, high noses and blond hair need some contrast, and so God gave them blue eyes, like two little ponds. Because American noses are so high their eyes are very deep; you have to peer in several miles to see their eyes! If they had black eyes at the bottom of such deep wells they would look fearful, almost evil in a way. Having lighter color eyes creates beauty and harmony in a much more dramatic way.

Imagine a person laughing whose teeth were all black. He would look like a monster! When you examine the creation you know that God is really an artist, and that no better harmony could have been created. Everything is interestingly blended, with people having precisely the features which would harmonize with a certain color face.

Light is always created at the boundary where two things meet in harmony. Why should people from one culture follow someone from an extremely different culture? Why have you Americans come to the Unification Church, which was founded by a man from Asia? You are here to unite the universal beauty of the two extremes of East and West together into one harmonized culture. When two great cultures meet to form harmony, turmoil is inevitable at first. When a flowing stream hits the rocks in its path, disturbances are created. It goes through many convolutions, splashing over rocks and churning at the bottom of a waterfall, but that does not alter its destiny. All streams eventually join the main stream which flows to the oceans.

There is tremendous variety and purity of creation in the mountains, and the water from mountain streams is also very healthy. Mountain water absorbs essences from the variety of creation found there, but rivers which run through the plains and flat lands, like the Mississippi or Nile, have no clean taste or special characteristics. Every pebble on the bottom of a mountain creek, every weed and every leaf, play an important part in harmonizing the entire environment. When looked at from this viewpoint everything becomes more beautiful. The running streams that start in the depths of the mountains will never make you sick, no matter how much you drink. Mountain animals drink the pure water and breathe clean air all the time, and so they are strong and healthy.

Everything that I am speaking of comes down to one simple word: harmony. The ideal world is not a world of uniformity and regimentation, but a world of harmony in which each person plays a distinctive role. It is not one species alone that creates the grandeur of the mountains. They are made beautiful in part by the infinite variety of the trees, some gigantic, some crooked, and of all different shades and hues.

The Unification of Religions

Here we are, products of the things that have happened to our ancestry. Here we are assembled—white people, yellow people, and black—but when we look back into the past, to the beginning of human history, we all started from one ancestry. Dividing into many streams, we have discriminated amongst ourselves. If we continue to be divided like this, when will the time come for us to be united again? There are so many historical events. We have been divided and sometimes united again by wars and by the ebb and flow of different cultural spheres.

When we think of religions, all religions have done great works. The religions have been transcending national boundaries and races because of their doctrines.

Many peoples have been united through religion. In the Christian world there have been so many different denominations, literally hundreds, but as a whole they have been bringing the world back to God.

There have been so many religions in the world, and each has its strengths and weaknesses. Thus, Buddhism teaches the need for mercy toward all living things, but it has not reached the core truth about God. Christianity has emphasized love, but without truly knowing love's essence, and without much sensitivity to nature. Nature is much more pure than humanity because it has preserved its original God-given nature, while human beings have distorted their original nature. Even people who live in great houses want to vacation at the beach, or go camping in the mountains. Their original form is looking for some comparable companion, and nature comes closest.

In the past God depended heavily upon many religions, but today's religions are in disarray, lacking discipline and direction. God's first problem is how to bring all religions into one unity so that they will serve the original purpose of religion and the practical work with which God has been concerned. Methodists may pray for Methodism to prosper, but that is only one of the 400 Christian denominations. Likewise for Presbyterians. God really feels the urge to jab them and say, "Stop that! Before you pray to me, make unity among all your fellow Christians. Then get together and pray to me. If you cannot unite the world, then at least you can unite with each other."

Christian denominations today, often promote their faith by proclaiming that their denomination alone can guarantee the Kingdom of Heaven. In God's sight this is a very unnecessary conflict. That blind, boastful attitude will bring nothing but their own decline and they will never see the sunlight. If there is truly a God of justice He would never let such churches prosper. He would be utterly disgusted.

However, imagine what could happen if Christians were crazy to gather all the denominations together and pray to relieve God's burden, asking God for the power and ability to reach out to the people. Then of course God would consider their prayer and do everything possible to answer it. God is waiting for the people on earth who will bring all these different denominations into one.

God never wanted division among people. He would like to see all humankind living together as one country. Americans might tell God to come live with them because after 200 years they have a very comfortable country for Him to live in; they might encourage Him to disregard other, struggling nations. Would God accept their invitation, or would He feel revolted by such thinking?

God would really be moved if people appeared on earth who would encourage Him to overlook the racial barriers separating people and the religious and cultural differences that humankind has fought over, and would demonstrate to Him that they were coming together to form one country centering on Him. America was right to adopt the motto "One nation under God," but it would have been better to teach "One world under God." America hasn't gotten that far yet. God's problem now is how to bring all nations into oneness.

God has nurtured civilizations and cultures, educating the generations in His way of thinking and living. It's not that religions are exclusive of each other, but that they are on different levels of development, such as the grade levels in a school system. Primitive religions are on a kindergarten level while others are at the grammar school level, and others the middle school or high school level. Some religions can be equated with the university standard. All religions are different in their degree of understanding of God. There are different subjects within a university and there are also different kinds of colleges. In religion as well we have to distinguish the different areas. For these reasons it makes absolutely no sense for one religion to fight with another religion. It shows they don't understand God or His work through religion.

Every Race Has Its Own God-Given Uniqueness

True love can transcend national boundaries or racial boundaries, and discrimination between religious sects. In this unity, we are all brothers and sisters. In the sight of God, there is no such thing as Orientals, Whites, and Blacks. Just think of the different colors—they are only our complexions. Because of the weather, because of geography, because of the situation from all your ancestral lines, we have different complexions. The climate caused that, but we are different only on the surface. Underneath, we come from the same God.

You cannot change the original form of things, because there is deep reasoning behind it. God had a reason for making things a certain way. So don't be proud of being handsome or ashamed of being ugly—there is no such thing as beautiful or ugly in God's sight. God always balances a person's features; if you have a wonderful face, you will have some deficiency elsewhere. A person who doesn't have beautiful features will have some other lovely aspect to balance that.

If you look in a garden, you see that the most gorgeous flowers don't last very long. A rose is beautiful and it lasts a long time, but has low-quality fragrance; noble, serene women don't wear such fragrance. The fantastic-looking flowers attract the insects all at once, and then fade. Beautiful women with strong attraction will not live a long time. Those with a beautiful face often have poor physical health in some way.

Since God is always thinking about balance, there is no one-sidedness in the world of His creation. Western eyelashes should be long to protect the eyes adequately. The Oriental eye is not as deep-set, and doesn't need such long eyelashes. Some Oriental women, thinking their short eyelashes are unseemly, wear artificial eyelashes, but to my thinking that is stupid and ugly looking. Also, instead of giving White people black or very dark eyes, He gave them blue or lighter-colored eyes, and the contrast between the iris and white of the eye is not as strong. But in Black and Oriental people who have very dark or black irises, the contrast is vivid and attractive.

In Black people, who have dark complexions, the whites of the eyes stand out beautifully; whereas in White people the contrast is not as strong. In laughter, when the pink tongue shows in between white teeth, the contrast is most vivid and sensational in Black people. For similar reasons, Black people have thicker lips. God gave balance by emphasizing certain characteristics in the different races, but the total result is equality.

In most cases today this civilization is trying to destroy or downplay certain original qualities in people, instead of trying to enhance them. But the time will come when White people will be crazy about Blacks. White women in particular will prefer the dramatic appearance of Black men.

In Western civilization, who has shed more sweat in building nations? Black people. White people are standing on top of it, but Blacks have shed more tears and sweat for it. Life germinates in fertile soil; it is not coincidence, then, that Black people are passionate and have an explosive sense of love. Also, they tend to trust people; since they represent the valley, they tend to embrace everything that washes down.

The White culture, coming from the top of the mountain, has held a dominant position of power, but everything eventually washes down to the valley. Whites represent a colder society, and White people are not as trusting. In movies you see White settlers moving west, and if their animals are sick or cannot go on the Whites kill them and move on. The Oriental nature could not do that; nor would Black people. Whites have a tradition of dueling for love, in which one man dies and the woman goes with the winner. Love cannot come through destruction of life; life must be nurtured to give love.

Have you Black members carried some kind of hidden grudge against White people? Black people can have two thoughts: one, that some day they will get revenge for injustice done them, or two, that they want to win the respect of White people by serving them and becoming one with them in love. For hundreds of years black people have been oppressed and enslaved, but can you forgive and forget that, and tell God you want to serve others regardless? Do you think you are superior or inferior to Whites? You are not different: you have two eyes and a nose and two ears, just like White people. The two races are just a different shade of color, one happening to be darker than the other.

A high mountaintop is always white and covered with snow, but in the valley the soil is always dark and fertile. Do animals always live on the top of the snow-capped mountain, or do they live in the fertile valleys instead? Black is a rich color; it has great depth, absorbing all the light. It is a very attractive and charming color. On the other hand, white is easily stained and hard to keep clean. It would be simple to cover the world with black, but much more difficult to make everything white.

Are there any schoolrooms where the teacher writes in black chalk on a white board? It would be crazy to use a white board. It would be impossible if you Blacks were trying to be white, to succeed even after a millennium, no matter who you prayed to. Instead of trying to be something else, take what you have and be proud of it. Whites, be proud. Blacks, be proud. Orientals, be proud. The precious metals of the earth don't lie on the surface, but deep within the dark earth, and you also have your dignity as Black men and women. Be proud of what you are. If your hope is that the entire world can be embraced in your arms, then you have the right idea.

Harmony between the Races

White and Black people live together here in America, but have they created perfect harmony in this land? Who is responsible for the lack of harmony, White, or Blacks? Be honest and frank. I agree with your answer than basically White people have been responsible. Even though God meant for harmony to exist when He put two extremes together, there is little harmony among the races here in America. The White people must take primary responsibility for the lack of harmony in this country.

At high noon the sun is bright, but even at that moment the sun is moving towards the opposite extreme of midnight. In living you must be willing to go through the darkness of midnight to arrive at the high noon of the next day. Western culture is primarily a White culture, and in general white people think of themselves as superior to Black and yellow people. Westerners think of their culture as being self-sufficient, but that is comparable to refusing to go through midnight; the sun cannot always remain at high noon. The West is now at evening time; it will never see broad daylight again unless there is unity. When westerners can be broadened by absorbing elements from other cultures, a new day will dawn and there will be the glorious prosperity of another high noon.

The Greek and Roman empires thought they could stay on the pinnacle forever. They had no intuition that they would be destroyed, but now their civilizations are gone. Today the Western culture is enjoying its ascendency, but this civilization will also terminate unless it seeks the valley. If white people keep on entertaining the idea of discrimination against black people, they will see a day of humiliation in their future because Black power and Yellow power will rise against them. In number, white people are only a third or less of the world population. Under the threat of communism, can anyone still entertain discrimination between the races?

If you have hated black people in the past, you should invite the ugliest, fattest Black man or grandmother to go out for lunch at a Chinese restaurant. Then over lunch you can say, "I have a confession to make. I have hated Black people, but now I want to love them." You can tell her how you felt in the past, but when you joined the Unification Church and met Rev. Moon you worked to train yourself as a champion of goodness. Now you repent, and as a sign of apology you sincerely brought her out to dinner. When you beg her with tears to eat the dinner you buy, you will have indemnified your hate in the past.

If someone has hated White people in the past then he also has to repent. Whatever you have bound in the past, you have to unbind now and indemnify it. If a man has been a playboy in the past and made many women sorrowful, he has to find some situation where he can apologize to one woman representing all of them. If a woman has married several times, then she has to apologize to a man in the same way. Everything you have done which was unprincipled you should indemnify.

In the Unification Church we are encouraging international marriages. Some people call me evil because of that, because I encourage an American boy to wed an Oriental girl. I can imagine the historical beauty of a white woman breast-feeding a black baby. That moment in history is beautiful.

People may not be able to understand me now, but after my death, even after centuries, people will understand that all the races, all the colors, must be mingled together. In God's sight all are brothers and sisters.

The Coming Cosmic Spring

Past history can be called a tropical culture. The cultures in India and Egypt all developed in hot weather. Twentieth century civilization can be compared to a climate of moderate weather. The past, as the summer, is now moving into an autumn culture in the 20th century. As the end of autumn weather brings winter, the culture of the West will be overtaken by the cold culture of the communist world.

When the winter comes, the leaves are blown away and no flowers blossom, yet even though the world looks gloomy, the plants still contain life within which will burst forth when the spring comes. During the cold weather the blossom of true love is waiting for its time, the coming of the cosmic spring. That is the ultimate culture to come for all humanity. No matter how severe the winter, once spring comes the winter has to give way.

Today's Western culture is equivalent to the autumn season, and no matter how much you may want to delay winter's arrival, its coming is inevitable. Even now winter is knocking at the door, and in order to be a fruitful seed, the Unification Church needs a shell of discipline and training that will enable it to survive under any circumstances. In summertime people go to cool places on their vacation, and in wintertime they go to warm places like Miami Beach, trying to escape the cold weather. But Unification Church members do the opposite: we meet the seasons head on and conquer them. That is our way of life. Your living that way is a manifestation of formidable spiritual power. The degree to which the American people say you are brainwashed is a measure of your conviction.

You know you will go through winter but you must also envision spring's coming. Your job is to make yourself a solid seed so that when the spring comes God will cast you on very fertile ground and you will be fruitful. Are you ready to be tested by the cold weather of communism? Could you withstand torture by people who want you to recant your faith? We have the hope that after the cold weather of communism passes a new world will be born and spring will come. That is the day our hope will be realized. The winter is never permanent. By gathering together people from all races and cultures we are trying to exchange each other's indestructible elements in order to arm ourselves to overcome any circumstance.

History is advancing toward one spring culture of the Kingdom of God on earth. That is the ultimate goal of human history. You are supposed to be the seed that will grow in that springtime, but where does a seed come from? God is the ultimate origin or root from which each seed grows. You are the seeds of God, created through the process of love, and two gigantic loves are essential for your life and must be harmonized within you — love of humanity and the love of God.

Spring is characterized by flowers blooming in color and fragrance. Blossoms should not be limited just to one race, but should be multi-colored, and that is what we are. That is why I have characterized the Unification Church as the love race. We are like gardeners cultivating a colorful garden, where the bees and butterflies come to enjoy the flowers, flitting from one to another. These are the people of the spirit world, and even God is coming. Would they discriminate about which color flower they go to? No, they enjoy the brilliance of them all.

The ideal civilization is the spring civilization. Throughout history man has thought that the ideal society with perfect love between humankind and God, and within humankind, was only a dream. But the Messiah will make the dream a reality. The Unification Church is born for that purpose and we can attain that goal. The greatest contribution we can make to the world is to knit all of humanity together with the love of God. Throughout history there has always been conflict between North and South, East and West, not just between nations but within families and on every level of society. Historically, unity has proved to be an impossible task, but I am striving for that today.

The Love of God Will Unite the World

Americans think you are just foolish young people, but wider acceptance of our movement will come when people see its fruit. The quickest way to unite humanity into one family is by intermarriage of the different races. The movement that can elevate such marriages will inevitably bring harmony and unity to the world, without war or conflict. In the future more and more Americans will seek international marriages uniting the different nations and races; these will bring honor, not shame.

To accomplish this gigantic historical task, you need to discover the extraordinary power of love, love that does not become the circumstantial victim of society. Supreme love transcends every national, racial and cultural barrier. People have always talked about love, but human love alone will never accomplish the task of universal unity. Therefore, the Unification Church rallies around one love, the love and heart of God. We are the first group in history to talk about the heart of God.

If it is really true that we know the heart of God, then we are like the sun rising in the morning, whose brightness will brighten the entire world. All humanity will be linked to the heart of God, which will spread all over the world and constantly pulse through the action of give and take, unable to stay in just one place. Once you harness the power of the heart of God, you will have the energy of a lightning bolt, lighting up all of America. You will feel, "I am the harmonizer of heavenly culture and earthly culture. I am the focal point of love. I am a messenger of the love of God, having the infinite energy that will bring springtime to this nation."

Let us pray.